M000030774

Especially for

....

From

....

Date

....

Peace
and
Comfort
for
Difficult Times

© 2015 by Barbour Publishing, Inc.

ISBN 978-1-64352-883-0

Published by Barbour Publishing, Inc., 1810 Barbour Drive, Uhrichsville, Ohio 44683, www.barbourbooks.com

Our mission is to inspire the world with the life-changing message of the Bible.

Member of the
Evangelical Christian
Publishers Association

Printed in China.

Peace
and
Comfort
for
Difficult Times

A Daily Devotional

BARBOUR

PUBLISHING

Introduction

This world is a dangerous place. No one comes through it untouched—not the dearest saint or the meanest sinner. But for those who put their trust in God, this world is just a temporary home. One day we will reside in heaven where love, joy, and peace prevail. Until then, He has promised us His comfort. No matter what we face in this lifetime, no matter what calamity comes our way—great or small—God has vowed never to let go of our hands.

Peace and Comfort for Difficult Times was created to remind you that you are never alone in your troubles. If you trust Him, He will be there in the good times and the bad, pouring out His love, providing wisdom and guidance, listening to your hurting heart, shouldering your burdens, and bringing you safely through to the other side.

Praise be to the God and Father of our Lord Jesus Christ. God is the Father who is full of mercy and all comfort. He comforts us every time we have trouble, so when others have trouble, we can comfort them with the same comfort God gives us.

2 Corinthians 1:3–4 ncv

Day 1
Everything He Has Given

Each of us will give a
personal account to God.

ROMANS 14:12 NLT

God holds us accountable for the many gifts He has given us, including our time and talents, our resources and relationships. Our heavenly Father, however, is not a heartless overseer with a checklist in hand, but a loving God who desires our ultimate happiness. He knows our joy, peace, and satisfaction increase when we explore our gifts to the fullest. For our benefit, God asks for accountability, inviting us to use wisely and well everything He has given.

Day 2
Adversity

"Do not fear or be dismayed:
tomorrow go out against them,
for the Lord is with you."

2 Chronicles 20:17 NKJV

Adversity, calamity, hardship, misfortune, trouble, hard times—no matter what you call them, these painful episodes are part and parcel of the human experience. But you can choose to not let them bring you down, fill you with fear, and steal your attention from the blessings God has placed in your life. Look adversity square in the eye and know that your God—the God of all comfort—has an answer.

Day 3
Ask Him

When I am surrounded by
troubles, you keep me safe.

PSALM 138:7 GNT

No matter how hard we work to avoid it, adversity rears its ugly head. It might be the result of a mistake we've made, but sometimes it's not our fault at all. Either way, the key to meeting adversity is not to dread it or fear it, but to believe in our God-given strength and abilities. Even in the middle of hardship, there is peace in knowing we can ask God for everything we need to overcome it.

Day 4
Never Alone

A friend loves at all times,
and a brother is born for adversity.

Proverbs 17:17 nkjv

When you give your heart and life to God, the Bible says Jesus Christ becomes your friend and your brother—and that changes everything. You aren't alone when adversity strikes. You've become a member of God's family and part of His circle of friends. His resources are marshaled in your defense, and His loving Holy Spirit—the Bible calls Him the Comforter—is with you constantly.

Day 5
Perspective

*[Jesus said,] "Come to Me,
all you who labor and are heavy laden,
and I will give you rest."*

MATTHEW 11:28 NKJV

"Stay calm!" For most of us, that's easier said than done when our situation turns bad. Yet "stay calm" is wise advice. By not reacting with panic, we give ourselves the perspective we need to assess our problem and sort through our options. That's why God assures us that He is with us and ready to help us at all times. With our trust placed in His strength and power, we're able to stay calm, even in adversity.

Day 6
Affliction

*The righteous person faces many troubles,
but the LORD comes to the rescue each time.*
PSALM 34:19 NLT

An affliction is any source of constant suffering in your life. That might be poverty or sickness or anxiety—only you know what you are facing. You may think that no one understands. But God does. No matter where you are, He's right there with you. Trust Him, and He will show you the way out, the way around, or the way through, and He will never leave your side.

Day 7
A Healing Balm

*Many are the afflictions of the righteous:
but the LORD delivereth him out of them all.*

PSALM 34:19 KJV

Many maladies are not physical, but spiritual. We might be afflicted with a timid nature, a nagging conscience, or a heavy heart. Perhaps we find ourselves prone to self-defeating behavior or to overdependence on others. While these afflictions may not be visible to other people, God sees, and He cares. The Great Physician of the spirit invites us to come to Him with whatever troubles us and receive the balm of His restorative touch.

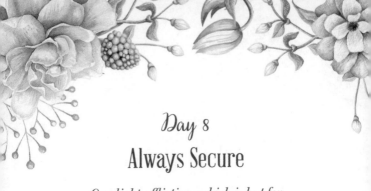

Day 8
Always Secure

Our light affliction, which is but for a moment, worketh for us a far more exceeding and eternal weight of glory.

2 Corinthians 4:17 kjv

Have you ever wondered why God doesn't just put an end to your troubles and give you a free pass from pain and suffering? After all, He can do anything! God doesn't bring suffering to your life, but sometimes He will ask you to walk through it for reasons known only to Him. But you can be sure of this—God will use your affliction to make you stronger and more secure in your faith.

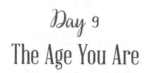

Day 9
The Age You Are

"I will be your God
throughout your lifetime—
until your hair is white with age."
ISAIAH 46:4 NLT

Growing up, most kids are eager to add another candle to their birthday cakes. Then all too soon, they'd rather not count candles at all anymore! Living at peace with the age we are begins with believing God has placed us in the world at the right time and in the right place to accomplish everything He has planned for us to do. Young, old, or in between, age is what we make of it!

Day 10
Agreement

All of you should be in agreement,
understanding each other, loving each
other as family, being kind and humble.

1 PETER 3:8 NCV

God knows that much of our strength and comfort comes from other people—our friends and loved ones. But what if there is no one in your life who can encourage and lift you, no one who can understand what you are going through, no one who can pray with you? Don't lose heart. Set yourself in agreement with God and His will for your life. As you agree with God, He will send others to agree with you.

Day 11
God-Given Passion

Do not let the sun go down while you are still angry,
and do not give the devil a foothold.

EPHESIANS 4:26–27

Anger, like fire, can either harm or help. Anger harms us when it smolders in our hearts and overwhelms us with bitterness. It harms others when it flares in verbal or physical violence. But anger helps us when it motivates us to warn others of danger, speak in defense of the innocent, and take a stand against injustice. Anger is a God-given passion intended to bring us closer to Him as we strive to work His goodness in the world.

Day 12
Complete Assurance

This is the confidence (the assurance, the privilege of boldness) which we have in Him: [we are sure] that if we ask anything (make any request) according to His will (in agreement with His own plan), He listens to and hears us.

1 JOHN 5:14 AMPC

What could be better than to be in full agreement with the One who knows the beginning from the end, someone who understands all the options and sees all the solutions? Take comfort in the fact that your prayer partner, your friend and comrade is God Himself. You can take any request to Him with the assurance that He will hear you. As you do, be sure to thank Him for His help.

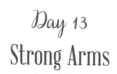

Day 13

Strong Arms

Cast all your anxiety on him,
because he cares for you.

1 PETER 5:7 NRSV

A physician once said to her patient, "It's not what you're eating; it's what's eating you." Unrelenting anxiety takes a toll on our physical and mental well-being, and that's why God invites us to give our worries to Him. He has strong arms, and He can hold anything we need to put in them. One by one, we must take each thing that burdens us and give it to God. Then we can relax, knowing He has our best interests at heart.

Day 14

Anxiety

*Cast all your anxiety on
him because he cares for you.*

1 Peter 5:7

This world gives us plenty of reasons to worry. Danger looms around every corner even for the wise and well-informed. People try all kinds of things to escape worry and anxiety—recreation, yoga, video games, sleep, to name just a few. But in the end there is only one sure remedy. God says to cast all your anxiety on Him. He's big enough to handle anything that comes your way.

Day 15
The Prayer Remedy

I want you to be free from anxieties.

1 CORINTHIANS 7:32 NRSV

God has a remedy for anxiety, and that remedy is prayer.
When we speak to Him about an issue that concerns us,
we are speaking to someone who has the power to do
something about it. Whether the issue is big or small,
a major problem or a minor annoyance, God's ear is
only a prayer away. The Great Physician longs to ease
our anxiety, embrace us in His comfort, and wrap our
hearts and minds in His peace.

Day 16
Cast Your Cares

Do not be anxious about anything, but in
every situation, by prayer and petition, with
thanksgiving, present your requests to God.
And the peace of God, which transcends
all understanding, will guard your hearts
and your minds in Christ Jesus.

PHILIPPIANS 4:6–7

What does it mean to "cast your care on God"? Start by opening your heart and telling Him about your fears, your worries, those things that make you feel anxious. Once you've done that, thank Him for taking all that worry off your hands. As you give up your anxious thoughts to Him, He gives you something back—His perfect peace.

Day 17

Delightful Beauty

God does not judge by
outward appearances.
GALATIANS 2:6 GNT

Many of us spend a lot of time in front of the mirror. We're quick to find fault with the smallest real or perceived blemish, and then our self-esteem takes a dive! Yet what's really important isn't outward appearance at all, but the appearance of our spirit: our character, our integrity, our compassion for others. While physical beauty fades, spiritual beauty lasts forever, and it's the kind of beauty God delights to see.

Day 18

Aspirations

*I do not mean that I am already as God wants
me to be. I have not yet reached that goal, but I
continue trying to reach it and to make it mine.*

PHILIPPIANS 3:12 NCV

Are you driven by that little voice inside you that keeps telling you to reach higher, try harder, and never give up until you attain a certain goal in your life? If your goal is within the scope of God's will, that voice is almost certainly His. It isn't His will for you to seek out temporal things like money, fame, or possessions. But He does want you to aspire to become everything He has created you to be.

Day 19
The Right Direction

*How joyful are those who fear the Lord
and delight in obeying his commands.*

Psalm 112:1 nlt

God's commandments are like curbs. Curbs are built to keep drivers on the road, and prevent them from swerving and endangering pedestrians. Similarly, when God tells us not to do something, He is doing so for our safety and for the safety of others. He says no to those things that would take us away from Him and the journey He has planned for us. It's His way of giving us the peace of knowing we're headed in the right direction.

Day 20
A Specific Plan

*"What matters most to me
is to finish what God started."*

ACTS 20:24 MSG

Who God wants you to be includes what He wants you to do. He has a specific plan for every single person in this world—including you. You may not have a grand talent or an extraordinary intellect, but you have been given everything you need to carry out your mission in life—your calling. Pray each day that God will help you find and complete the work He has given you to do.

Day 21
Guiding Others

There is no authority except from God.
ROMANS 13:1 NKJV

Many of us are uncomfortable with authority. We may shy away from imposing rules on children in the home or fail to articulate our wishes to subordinates in the workplace. When God places us in positions of authority, however, He is entrusting us with the privilege of guiding others in the same way He guides us, and that is with compassion, kindness, and understanding. Authority is ours not to build up ourselves, but to build up others in love.

Day 22

Assurance

Faith is the assurance of things hoped for.
HEBREWS 11:1 NASB

We human beings have plenty of insecurities, so you shouldn't be ashamed to admit you have a few. The good news is that you don't have to let them shape your life. When you place your faith in God, they will be replaced by the steadfast assurance that those things you hope for are yours through His love and grace. No more wondering if you're good enough or lovable enough or smart enough. In God's eyes you are perfect.

Day 23
Comfort

Yea, though I walk through the valley of the shadow
of death, I will fear no evil; for You are with me;
Your rod and Your staff, they comfort me.

PSALM 23:4 NKJV

When we lose someone we love, the pain cuts deep.
Sometimes it last for years; and even after decades have
passed, the wound still aches. Right where it hurts is
where God desires to soothe and comfort us. He yearns
to assure us of His continuing presence in our lives,
and to strengthen us with confidence in His unfailing
wisdom in all things. Even in the depths of loss, our
peace rests with Him.

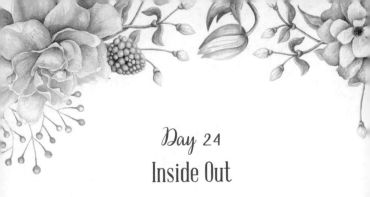

Day 24
Inside Out

My flesh and my heart may fail, but God is the strength of my heart and my portion forever.

God has everything under control. That's not just a pie-in-the-sky concept—it's a fact. God knows and understands you from the inside out. And when you place your life in His hands, you can be certain that in the good times and the bad times, the happy times and the heartbreaking times, you will always have someone to depend on, someone to fall back on, someone stronger than any challenge you could possibly face.

Day 25
An Invitation

*Don't let anyone become bitter and
cause trouble for the rest of you.*

HEBREWS 12:15 CEV

Drop a speck of dirt into a glass of clean water, and the
water is no longer fit to drink. Dirt and purity cannot
coexist, and neither can bitterness and peace of mind.
That's why God invites us to come to Him with whatever
makes us feel the least bit bitter, whether it's memories
from long ago or circumstances in our lives right now.
He longs to replace bitterness with blessings, resentment
with rest, and anger with peace.

Day 26
Battles

Sovereign LORD, my strong deliverer,
you shield my head in the day of battle.

PSALM 140:7

You may be facing a battle right now—a fight for your health, your children, your finances, for example. As the battle rages, know that you are not facing the enemy alone. Your God is fighting by your side. He is leading the charge to bring you safely through. Put your confidence in Him. Follow His lead, and let His unmatched strength be a comfort to you.

Day 27

A Cooling Pool of Forgiveness

*Get rid of all bitterness, passion,
and anger. No more shouting or insults,
no more hateful feelings of any sort.*

Ephesians 4:31 GNT

Few stories inspire more than those about women and men who have refused to let injustice rob them of their dignity. Rather than bathe in hate and bitterness, they refreshed themselves in the cooling pool of forgiveness. They have discovered how to live at peace even in the face of unfairness and undeserved animosity. It's God's way, and it's what we discover when we let His Spirit replace our bitterness with His forgiveness, our hurt with His understanding.

Day 28
Carried

*It is God who arms me with strength and keeps my
way secure. He makes my feet like the feet of a deer;
he causes me to stand on the heights. He trains my
hands for battle; my arms can bend a bow of bronze.*

PSALM 18:32–34

It could be that you have been battling for so long that
you are feeling weak, exhausted, and ready to throw in
the towel. Close your eyes and rest your troubled mind.
Don't worry, even when you're resting, God and His
army are still fighting on your behalf, and they won't stop
until the battle is won. It's all right to take a break and
let Him carry you for a while.

Day 29
Making Things Right

*[Jesus said,] "Do not judge, and you
will not be judged; do not condemn,
and you will not be condemned."*

LUKE 6:37 NRSV

When things go wrong, we want to find out why. In our search, however, we're often distracted by pointing a finger at other people, and it's then that we lose the chance to learn from our mistakes. If we let Him, God will gently shift our search inward, and lead us to a deeper understanding of our motives and desires, attitude and actions. From there we can step forward in peace to make things right again.

Day 30
Beauty

*Don't be concerned about the outward beauty
of fancy hairstyles, expensive jewelry, or beautiful
clothes. You should clothe yourselves instead with the
beauty that comes from within, the unfading beauty of
a gentle and quiet spirit, which is so precious to God.*

1 PETER 3:3–4 NLT

Twenty-first-century women are exposed to an almost impossible standard of beauty. And the message is unrelenting. In such an environment, every little flaw or blemish can be devastating. God says that outward beauty is of no consequence unless there is beauty on the inside. After all, even the most beautiful woman cannot hope to keep her looks for long. The beautiful, godly soul, however, lives forever.

Day 31
God's Embrace

*Before the world was created, God had Christ
choose us to live with him and to be his holy
and innocent and loving people.*

EPHESIANS 1:4 CEV

"What did I do wrong?" From those plaintive words
flows a stream of self-blame for the rebelliousness of a
child, faithlessness of a spouse, or betrayal of a friend.
It's called a guilt trip, and it's a journey God doesn't
want us to take. Instead, He asks us to go no further
than His embrace, where He will listen as we pour out
our hearts to Him. Let Him show the way to genuine
acceptance and spiritual peace.

Day 32
Intention and Purpose

*"The Lord does not look at the things people look at.
People look at the outward appearance,
but the Lord looks at the heart."*

1 Samuel 16:7

Who says what is beautiful and what is not? It would seem that the creator of a work of art would be the one whose opinion matters most. For the creator, every nuance, every brushstroke, every indention in the clay has meaning. God created you—with intention and purpose. You are His work of art. In His eyes, you are beautiful in every way, inside and out.

Day 33
Never the Same

The Lord is close to the brokenhearted;
he rescues those whose spirits are crushed.

PSALM 34:18 NLT

Life will never be the same again, of that we are sure. While God doesn't promise to shield our hearts from all pain, He does promise to fill our hearts with His comfort. He is a God eager to heal and to put back together what has been broken by sin or sorrow. No, we may never understand why it happened on this side of heaven, but we can accept it. We may never be the same, but we can live at peace.

Day 34
Belief

*Once made perfect, [Jesus] became the source
of eternal salvation for all who obey him.*

HEBREWS 5:9

The older we are the more we understand the futility of
this life. But there is great comfort in knowing that this
life is not the end. Through His Son, Jesus Christ, God
has provided a remedy for sin, with its constant menu
of corruption and death. No longer are we headed only
for the grave—but to the grave and beyond. This sacred
belief is our blessed hope.

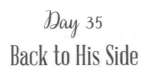

Day 35

Back to His Side

The LORD God is waiting to show how kind he is and to have pity on you. The LORD always does right; he blesses those who trust him.

ISAIAH 30:18 CEV

A broken heart is a mark of love, for only those we love have the power to grieve us. Because God loves us beyond measure, He knows what a broken heart feels like, for we have often strayed away from Him. Yes, we have the power to grieve Him, but He has the power and the will to bring us back to His side. God is ready to mend the rift between Himself and the sorrowful soul.

Day 36

Life Everlasting

Jesus said to her, "I am the resurrection and the life. The one who believes in me will live, even though they die; and whoever lives by believing in me will never die. Do you believe this?"

John 11:25–26

Your beliefs say a lot about your future. For example, believing that hard work leads to success will help you meet your goals. Believing that true love lasts forever will help you remain steadfast in your marriage. And believing that God has promised you life everlasting will allow you to continue to value yourself even as your body ages and your earthly life winds down. Beliefs are important, and those invested in God pay the biggest dividends of all.

Day 37
A Smooth Way Ahead

*Since we are living by the Spirit, let us follow the
Spirit's leading in every part of our lives.*

GALATIANS 5:25 NLT

Change leads to anything but tranquility! Any significant
life change, even a welcome one, produces stress until a
new level of comfort and familiarity sets in. When we face
change, we must allow God to smooth the way ahead
and show us His will. After all, there's no place we're
going that He hasn't been. Whether the path ahead looks
exciting or scary, we can step forward with confidence,
knowing our God is walking right beside us.

Day 38

Belonging

You are all the same in Christ Jesus.
You belong to Christ.
GALATIANS 3:28–29 NCV

We all want to belong. It's a normal human instinct. Unfortunately, our culture places value on so many things that have no lasting meaning—where we live, how we dress, where our children go to school. Comfort yourself with the truth that God values you for who you really are deep inside, nothing more, nothing less. You are His magnificent creation and a member of His royal family. You belong to Him.

Day 39
What Bliss!

Jesus Christ the same yesterday,
and to day, and for ever.

HEBREWS 13:8 KJV

In a world of constant change, what comfort to know that God never changes! From the beginning of time, His love for the world has endured, and nothing we could do will ever alter His love. His promises remain as valid as they were when He first spoke them, and His desire to bring us closer to Him still burns within His unchangeable heart. From the turmoil of change to the peace of God's presence—what bliss!

Day 40
Abandonment

Whether we live or die,
we belong to the Lord.

ROMANS 14:8

Have you ever been abandoned by a friend or family member? There are few feelings worse than a lost relationship. That's why it's so important to know that once you belong to the Lord, you will always belong to Him. Even when you mess up and make poor choices, your heavenly Father will not abandon you. For the remainder of this life and the life to come—you are His!

Day 41
The Next Generation

*Train children in the right way,
and when old, they will not stray.*

PROVERBS 22:6 NRSV

Whether or not we have children of our own, we are setting an example for the young. If there are children in our homes, they learn from us how to get along in the world—not so much from what we tell them, but from what they see us do. In public places, young people take their cue from the attitude and behavior of the adults around them. Spiritually, each of us is a "mother" to the next generation.

Day 42

Bereavement

*[Jesus said,] "Blessed are those who mourn,
for they will be comforted."*

MATTHEW 5:4

Losing someone you love is one of the most devastating experiences in life—whether that is a friend or relative, your child or your spouse, even a beloved pet who has brightened your life and helped ward off loneliness. God understands your grief. He gave up His own precious Son for you. He knows the anguish of losing someone who meant everything to Him. Let Him comfort you as only He can.

Day 43
Excellence

I run with purpose in every step.
I am not just shadowboxing.

1 CORINTHIANS 9:26 NLT

If we believe competition is all about the thrill of victory and the agony of defeat, it's no wonder we might decide not to compete with others! But when we compete with ourselves to excel at what we do, to advance on our spiritual journey, and to walk closer with God every day, then we have the right idea about competition. Seen God's way, competition motivates us to become more and more the peace-loving women He intends us to be.

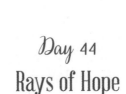

Day 44

Rays of Hope

He will swallow up death forever. The Sovereign
LORD will wipe away the tears from all faces.

ISAIAH 25:8

When you lose someone you love, you might wonder what possible comfort anyone could give you—even God. But there is comfort in looking beyond the grave, beyond this life, and knowing that your separation from that beloved one, while excruciating, is not permanent. The two of you will meet again in a place where death no longer has meaning. Even in the darkest moments, God lights your way with hope.

Day 45
Conflict Resolution

*A truly wise person uses few words; a person
with understanding is even-tempered.*

PROVERBS 17:27 NLT

In conflicts, emotions take over. Though we might face
our foes with steely resolve, inside we're a knot of nerves;
or we're so upset that we simply run from the fight! God
has a better way. Godly conflict resolution begins with
one person letting go of emotions and approaching
the other with reason, understanding, and a will to
compromise. It ends in peace, with a deeper relationship
based on genuine caring and mutual respect.

Day 46
Betrayal

*He will shelter you with his wings. His faithful
promises are your armor and protection.*

PSALM 91:4 NLT

Betrayal is such a bitter word. It's always personal. You
invested yourself in someone and that person purpose-
fully turned away. Whenever you place your trust in a
human being, you risk betrayal. We just don't have the
wherewithal to remain 100 percent faithful. But God
does. And He promises never to betray the trust you
place in Him. He'll even be there to pick up the pieces,
to comfort you, when others fail you.

Day 47

A Closer Walk

*"No person can steal my sheep
out of my Father's hand."*

JOHN 10:29 NCV

Perhaps the most intense conflict we will ever experience won't be with someone else, but with ourselves. In our continuing desire to walk closer to God, we battle emotions, thoughts, and temptations that throw us into turmoil. But we do not confront these enemies of faith alone because God's Spirit fights alongside us and for us. No matter how intense the struggle, we must hold to the peace of knowing our God will prevail.

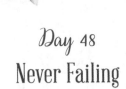

Day 48
Never Failing

"I'll marry you for good—forever! I'll marry you
true and proper, in love and tenderness. Yes, I'll
marry you and neither leave you nor let you go.
You'll know me, GOD, for who I really am."

HOSEA 2:19–20 MSG

No other betrayal is quite as painful as the loss of marital love and fidelity. All those bright promises of happily ever after lay broken in the dust. If you're feeling this closest of all betrayals, God wants to comfort you with His proposal. He wants to serve as your spiritual husband, providing you with the love, faithfulness, compassion, guidance, understanding, and caring you so desperately need. He won't fail you.

Day 49
God's Scales

Godliness with contentment is great gain.
1 TIMOTHY 6:6 KJV

When it comes to evaluating our lives, God's scales weigh differently than ours. The smallest of things can bring us the deepest joy. When we embrace our lives just as they are, we can lay down the struggle for what might be or might have been. We can discover the blessing of contentment, knowing that, for this moment, our lives are the perfect starting place for the next step in the journey.

Day 50

Boldness

[Jesus has] been through weakness and testing, experienced it all—all but the sin. So let's walk right up to him and get what he is so ready to give. Take the mercy, accept the help.

<small>HEBREWS 4:15–16 MSG</small>

God is big and powerful and holy. Even the most impressive woman pales in His shadow. Good sense would dictate that we keep our distance, interacting only when we are out of options. But in this case, good sense takes a backseat to God's ways. He has invited us to be bold with our requests, comfortable in His presence. He has called us His children. What a wonderful privilege!

Day 51

Enough!

*I have learned to be content
with whatever I have.*

PHILIPPIANS 4:11 NRSV

Having what we want, or wanting what we have. It's amazing the difference in simply reordering the words! What a gift it is to feel that sense of *enough*, to not always be thinking *more*, to believe that God has given what we truly need. As we focus today on the pockets of our lives that we "wouldn't have any other way," let's whisper a prayer of thanks. Take a breath and let this moment be full, just on its own.

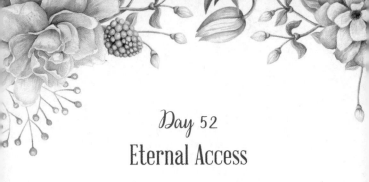

Day 52
Eternal Access

*In Christ we can come before God
with freedom and without fear.
We can do this through faith in Christ.*

EPHESIANS 3:12 NCV

Our boldness before God resides in His authority, not in our own. He has set the stage for our adoption as His children, heirs to blessing and eternal life. Our part is simply to accept, to say "yes" and take our places around His table. Through faith in His love and grace, we gain bold access to His presence. Once you place your faith in who He is, you will know who you are.

Day 53

When We Need It

Lord, you are my shield, my wonderful
God who gives me courage.

Psalm 3:3 NCV

We never know where courage will pop up in our lives, because we never know what we'll face that will require it. We can be sure, though, that God will give us courage when we need it. God is both our protector and our strength. So we can be confident that whatever we face, we do not face it alone. We face today with resources both from our own souls and the Spirit that dwells within us.

Day 54
Broken Heart

The LORD is close to the brokenhearted
and saves those who are crushed in spirit.

PSALM 34:18

God's love is manifest at all times in our lives, but never
so much as when our hearts are breaking. It is then that
we experience His compassion and comfort in ways
we cannot even imagine during the good times. When
you've suffered a betrayal or loss or disappointment,
when life threatens to bury you under the cold, hard
ground, God is there with hope and comfort in your
darkest hour.

Day 55
Victory Is Waiting

[Jesus said,] "Take heart,
because I have overcome the world."

JOHN 16:33 NLT

While living in this world that we can touch and see, we remember that we are also part of a world that we know only through faith. In the physical world around us, there's disappointment and struggle, for sure. But as citizens of the kingdom of heaven, we know a greater power that advocates for us. Jesus never claimed we would be without struggle, but He always reminded His followers of the victory that is waiting.

Day 56

Precious Tears

[God] heals the brokenhearted
and binds up their wounds.

PSALM 147:3

God has promised to see you through the most painful hours of your life, but His love and compassion don't end there. If you let Him, He will pick up the pieces of your broken heart and put them back together again. Your tears are precious to your heavenly Father, your suffering never wasted. You can trust Him to understand your sorrow—even enter into it with you—as He brings healing and new life from the ashes.

Day 57

Spiritual Sweetness

Don't mistreat someone who has mistreated you.
But try to earn the respect of others, and do
your best to live at peace with everyone.

ROMANS 12:17–18 CEV

When we're working among others either at our job or elsewhere, we bring our emotions with us. Inevitably, we hear a hurtful remark or feel slighted by someone else, and our relationship with the group suffers. And so do we. God changes our bitter feelings to spiritual sweetness when we respond with composure, overlooking offenses and granting friendliness, kindness, and respect. Even if peace doesn't reign among others, it can reign in us.

Day 58
Eternal Work

"Do not work for food that spoils, but for
food that endures to eternal life, which the
Son of Man will give you. For on him God
the Father has placed his seal of approval."

JOHN 6:27

All of us must work for the food that sustains our lives
here on earth. But God would remind us that we should
work for our spiritual food as well. The Bible says that
Jesus is the Bread of Life. Your relationship with Him
provides you with food for your spirit, food like wisdom,
understanding, insight, and counsel—food like joy,
peace, love, and patience. Work hard to provide your
spirit with all the spiritual food it needs.

Day 59
Called to Action

*Be ready at all times to answer anyone who
asks you to explain the hope you have in you.*

1 PETER 3:15 GNT

Most of us find it easier to contemplate God's commandments than to practice them. Yet we're called to action, and what better place to start than with and among the people we work with every day? They're the ones who will notice our willingness to go the extra mile, our peacefulness in tense situations, our self-control under fire, and our respect for everyone. Our coworkers are the ones who may ask how they too could walk with God.

Day 60
Burdens

Praise be to the Lord, to God our Savior,
who daily bears our burdens.

PSALM 68:19

Women are burden-carriers of the first order. In addition to our own responsibilities and troubles, we often take on those of others. God says, "You can't carry all that by yourself. Let Me help." Then He comes up alongside and helps us shoulder the load. If you feel you are faltering beneath your burdens, tell Him you are ready to let Him lend a hand. He won't touch your stuff unless you ask Him. But when you do, He'll step right up.

Day 61
Important Issues

Whoever heeds life-giving correction will be at home among the wise. Those who disregard discipline despise themselves, but the one who heeds correction gains understanding.

PROVERBS 15:31–32

When someone criticizes us, it's only natural for us to feel hurt and upset. But what did we actually hear—a mean-spirited opinion or an uncomfortable fact? To find out usually requires soul searching, prayer, and perhaps consultation with a trustworthy friend or family member. Once we understand the spirit behind the criticism, peace is ours. We can dismiss the remark or thank the person who cares about us enough to bring an important issue to our attention.

Day 62
Solutions Provided

*"Come to me, all of you who are weary and
carry heavy burdens, and I will give you rest."*
MATTHEW 11:28 NLT

God isn't going to snap His fingers and make your
financial woes disappear. You will still have to deal with
your problem children and bear responsibility for your
aging parents or your boss's unrealistic expectations.
But God will faithfully provide solutions, like help
from other human hands, wisdom, and counsel. And
He'll give you a place of rest along the way—like a well-
watered oasis in the desert.

Day 63
God's Truth

We will speak the truth in love.
EPHESIANS 4:15 NLT

Should we speak up or butt out? Yes, God would have us warn others to keep them from harm, and yes, He would have us resist the temptation to meddle in others' affairs. We can discern His will by knowing our motivation. Is it to bring God's truth to a straying person, or to bolster our own ego at the expense of someone else? After we've answered that question, we know exactly what God would have us do.

Day 64

Challenges

*Just as the sufferings of Christ flow
over into our lives, so also through
Christ our comfort overflows.*

2 CORINTHIANS 1:5

Are you facing an extreme challenge in your life—perhaps your children are rebelling, your marriage is floundering, your health is in peril, your finances are out of control? Jesus had challenges as well—big ones. He was subjected to all manner of indignities, pain, and suffering. Although He submitted Himself to those cruel circumstances for our sake, in God's perfect time He rose up and conquered both sin and death.

Day 65
Deeper and Deeper

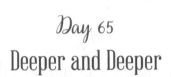

Just as you received Christ Jesus as Lord, continue to live your lives in him, rooted and built up in him, strengthened in the faith as you were taught.

Colossians 2:6–7

We walk our spiritual walk, day after day, sometimes unsure of our progress. Nevertheless, the roots are going down. We can't see beneath the soil where God tends to our faith, but the longer we continue in the direction of faith, the deeper His hold on us. We came to Him with nothing to use as a bargaining chip, just acceptance of His love. And that is all it takes to keep walking and growing deeper and deeper.

Day 66
Challenges Conquered

Because the Sovereign LORD helps me, I will not be disgraced. Therefore have I set my face like flint, and I know I will not be put to shame.

ISAIAH 50:7

Even though God uses certain negative situations in our lives to strengthen and equip us, He doesn't cause our adverse circumstances. Most often they are the result of our own poor choices or the poor choices of others. Ask God to accomplish His will in your life and then help you rise up and conquer your challenges—just as Jesus did.

Day 67

His Daughter

What does the LORD require of you? To act justly and
to love mercy and to walk humbly with your God.

MICAH 6:8

Day by day, the woman of God calmly and joyfully
goes about her work. She never frets about making
it to the top, for God asks only that she do her best.
She's not distraught if she doesn't win, for God asks
only for her faithfulness. She pays no attention to what
others think of her or her place in the world, for God
has called her His daughter and blesses every day of
her life with His love.

Day 68

Children

This is what the Lord says: . . . "I will
comfort you as a mother comforts her child."
Isaiah 66:12–13 ncv

Raising children is the most difficult, rewarding, exhausting, beautiful, chaotic, amazing job a woman can have. It's a mixed bag of dynamic emotions, pure affections, and unwavering devotion. When her children need comfort, a true mother instinctively provides it. God is the same way with His children. When you are hurting, He is there without fail, reaching out to you.

Day 69
Danger Detour

I beg you to avoid the evil things your bodies
want to do that fight against your soul.

1 PETER 2:11 NCV

Like a flashing red light on the roadway, danger signals from God warn us of peril ahead. His signals may come as a troubled conscience, a nagging suspicion that our conduct needs correction, or a particular verse from the Bible that speaks to us at gut-deep level. We avoid calamity by heeding His signal immediately! He will restore our peace of mind and heart as we stop, pray, and listen, and then follow His detour around the hazard.

Day 70
Confidence

In the fear of the LORD there is strong confidence.
PROVERBS 14:26 NKJV

Everywhere we look there are messages about how to be filled with inner confidence. Take this course, dress this way, speak your mind, and the ever-popular suggestion to reach down deep inside yourself. Unfortunately, those tactics only give the illusion of confidence. True confidence comes from knowing that almighty God, the creator and sustainer of the universe, is backing you up and showing you the way.

Day 71
Peace of Mind

"Do not lie. Do not deceive one another."
LEVITICUS 19:11

Most of us know what it's like to be deceived by someone. Not only are we angry at the deceiver, but we're angry at ourselves for believing the person in the first place! Forgiveness for the deceiver, however, opens the way to forgiveness for ourselves. Then we can possess the peace of mind and heart necessary to face forward, using our experience to warn others and shield ourselves against any future deceptive designs.

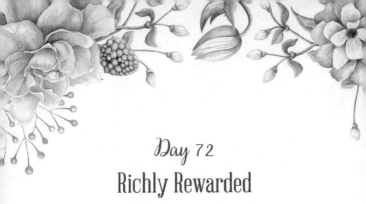

Day 72

Richly Rewarded

Do not throw away your confidence;
it will be richly rewarded.

HEBREWS 10:35

Circumstances of life often tend to erode our confidence
and leave us feeling weak and unproductive. When
you encounter those times, don't throw away your
confidence—redirect it. Make sure that it is anchored in
God's character, resources, and unwavering faithfulness.
People will fail you, and you will even fail yourself at
times, but God will never let you down.

Day 73

Creator of Time

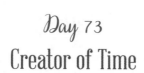

Wait for the promise of the Father.

ACTS 1:4 KJV

Most of us do not like delay! We fidget in waiting rooms and grocery lines, and when we send a friend a text, we're annoyed if she doesn't respond immediately. Yes, that's us. But God is the creator of time, He knows time from its beginning to its end, and He knows where in time to grant the blessing we so earnestly desire. We pray, and wait with faith, trusting Him to say, "The time is now."

Day 74
Creativity

*For in him all things were created: things in
heaven and on earth, visible and invisible,
whether thrones or powers or rulers or authorities;
all things were created through him and for him.*

COLOSSIANS 1:16

God is quite the Master Artist, and He takes His
work seriously. You may have noticed the delicious
burnt umber of the sunset, the yellow-green waters of
Lake Superior, or a towering stand of timber. Yes,
that was His work. The entire universe is His gallery.
But those spectacular pieces are little more than
eye candy compared to His human creations. God
expressed His extraordinary creativity when He created
you—and He calls you His best work.

Day 75
God-Given Delay

*Be patient and wait for the L*ORD *to act.*
PSALM 37:7 GNT

Most all of us can name a special thing we'd like to do "someday." And the reason we aren't doing it today is because we have other, higher priorities that need our attention. Our willingness to accept delay shows that we accept God's timing for our lives and know the value of postponing those things better suited to a future year, as He wills. In faith, we can embrace God-given delay with ease and confidence.

Day 76

A Creative Bent

So God created human beings in his own image.
In the image of God he created them;
male and female he created them.

GENESIS 1:27 NLT

Did you know you were created in God's image? No wonder you feel that urge to create. Don't hold back. Open your mind to new thoughts, new mental pictures, new ways of doing things. Ask God to open wide the gates of your creativity. You may not be an artist or a musician or a writer, but God has given each person—including you—a creative bent, and He is anxious for you to find yours.

Day 77

Lean on Him

"Do not be worried and upset," Jesus told them.
"Believe in God and believe also in me."

JOHN 14:1 GNT

It's possible to hide the symptoms of depression behind a brave face or a casual "I'm good" in reply to those who ask. But God, who searches the heart, can see the shadows of sadness that sap our strength and wear away at our happiness. He looks at us with mercy and compassion rather than judgment. He opens His arms to us and invites us to lean on Him as He soothes, heals, and comforts our hurting hearts.

Day 78

Danger

*"Whoever listens to me will live in safety
and be at ease, without fear of harm."*

PROVERBS 1:33

Remember the Ten Commandments? Many people think making those rules was God's way of asserting His authority, making sure we all know He's in charge. But a closer look shows that He is more interested in keeping us safe in a dangerous world. Just as you institute guidelines to keep your children out of harm's way, our loving heavenly Father has done the same.

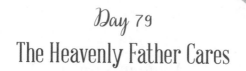

Day 79

The Heavenly Father Cares

*"I am the LORD your God; I strengthen you and
tell you, 'Do not be afraid; I will help you.'"*

<small>ISAIAH 41:13 GNT</small>

Depression can hit anyone, and it can hit hard. Whether
we can trace it to a specific incident or not, depression's
darkness can envelop us for days, weeks, or even longer.
It's nothing to be ashamed of, and it's nothing to ignore.
We all have people in our lives who can and will help,
if given the chance. If we don't have family or friends
nearby, we can take advantage of resources in our
communities. And no matter where we are, there is our
heavenly Father, who knows, understands, and cares.

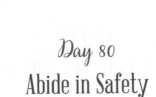

Day 80

Abide in Safety

The wise see danger ahead and avoid it.

PROVERBS 27:12 NCV

It probably isn't possible to avoid all danger in this treacherous world, but living wisely and paying attention to God's Word can give you a real advantage. Parents often establish rules for their family that the kids don't understand. But parents know the rules are for the kids' safety and well-being. Sometimes you won't see the reason for God's rules either, but obeying them will help you skirt danger and abide in safety.

Day 81

Surprised and Amazed

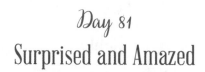

*"Anyone who trusts in me
will not be disappointed."*

ISAIAH 49:23 NCV

As we spend more time thinking about God, we become aware of His work in our lives. Certain changes, openings, and opportunities that come our way leave us feeling surprised and amazed. When we open our eyes to all the blessings He has showered on us, our hearts fill with wonder and gratitude. As we walk closer and closer with Him, there's one feeling we'll never have to worry about—disappointment!

Day 82
Debt

Let no debt remain outstanding,
except the continuing debt to love one other.
ROMANS 13:8

It's rare to find anyone in our current culture who is truly debt free. Financial advisors even contend that some calculated debt is an advantage. The trouble is that debt can quickly spiral out of control. If you're facing a mountain of debt each month you know how hopeless it feels. God wants you to be free—free to fulfill your destiny. If you ask Him, He'll help you find a plan to free yourself.

Day 83

Every Step

"God blesses those who mourn,
for they will be comforted."

<small>MATTHEW 5:4 NLT</small>

When we don't reach the goals we set for ourselves, we often feel disappointment. Though God may use it to turn us toward Him and His will for our lives, He warns against letting disappointment turn us away from a worthy, God-given dream. Instead, He desires to help us, strengthen us, and encourage us. Like a personal life coach, God wants us to succeed, and He will remain with us every step of the way.

Day 84
Good Habits

*God called you to be free, but do not
use your freedom as an excuse to do
what pleases your sinful self.*

GALATIANS 5:13 NCV

Freeing yourself from debt will take some work. It may mean sacrifices, changing your way of doing things, replacing bad habits with good ones. But you can be sure that God will be behind you all the way. He'll provide comfort, wisdom, and encouragement along the way. He'll even give you favor with your creditors. And the day you wake up and realize you are free will be worth it all.

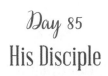

Day 85

His Disciple

*Jesus said, "If you hold to my teaching,
you are really my disciples. Then you will know
the truth, and the truth will set you free."*

<small>JOHN 8:31–32</small>

We may not call ourselves disciples, but we are. The question God poses is this: What are we disciples of? To answer honestly, many women would have to say romance or security, money or beauty. Each person has to decide for herself. God invites us to become His disciple. Our "yes" means we put Him first in all things. It means we walk in peace and contentment with our trust in Him. This is the kind of discipleship God has called us to.

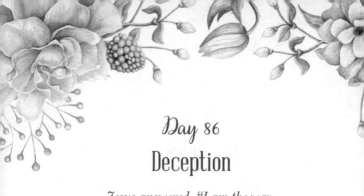

Day 86

Deception

*Jesus answered, "I am the way,
and the truth, and the life. The only
way to the Father is through me."*

John 14:6 NCV

If you've ever been deceived, you know how devastating it can be. Not only do you feel hurt, but your sense of trust is shaken as well. Maybe that's why God so often reminds us in the Bible that He represents truth, pure and simple. There is no deception in Him. He won't try to secure your love with empty promises. He can be trusted. Wrap your heart and mind around that truth and let it heal you.

Day 87
Walking with God

I am persuaded that neither death nor life. . .
nor height nor depth, nor any other created thing,
shall be able to separate us from the love of God.

ROMANS 8:38–39 NKJV

Our walk with God puts us in discipleship with Him. The blessing of discipleship, however, won't keep us from experiencing the bumps along the road, like ridicule or scorn, hardship or even persecution that comes as a result of our faith. And those things too are a blessing, because in them we know our discipleship is showing! Discipleship means we know we will never be without His presence and love, no matter how many twists and turns we encounter on the road ahead.

Day 88
Filled with Truth

*The heart is deceitful above all things and
beyond cure. Who can understand it?*

JEREMIAH 17:9

God knows we are vulnerable to deception not only
from others but also from our own hearts. We humans
have an innate inclination to lie to ourselves. But God
has a remedy. He encourages us to follow Him, listen to
Him, trust His words. Can you trust your heart? The
sweet Holy Spirit—the Comforter—will help you keep
your heart clean and filled with truth.

Day 89
The Road Uphill

*"Be strong and courageous! Do not
be afraid or discouraged. For the LORD
your God is with you wherever you go."*

JOSHUA 1:9 NLT

Sometimes it feels like we're climbing uphill all the way, making little or no progress. We are encouraged when we realize we aren't alone, that many women are feeling exactly the way we're feeling. When we reach out to friends and loved ones, we can do so knowing they will understand. And we can return the favor when others look to us, when they need someone to care. The road uphill is easier when we walk hand in hand with others, and with God.

Day 90
Defeat

We have troubles all around us, but we
are not defeated. We do not know what
to do, but we do not give up the hope of living.

2 CORINTHIANS 4:8 NCV

Sometimes it seems like one little thing goes wrong, and it starts a chain reaction of disappointments and negative expectations. The power of this process is in its cumulative nature. Like the straw that breaks the camel's back, one defeat sits on another until it brings us down. God says His mercies are new every morning. Each day is a new beginning. He wants us to put our troubles behind us and cling to the hope of living.

Day 91
God's Mighty Power

The Lord. . .will always be with you and help you,
so don't ever be afraid of your enemies.
DEUTERONOMY 31:8 CEV

Sometimes we're discouraged because we're focused on what stands against us. The obstacles are huge, and we consider ourselves realistic to call them exactly what they are. But if we stop there, we're ignoring God's mighty power. It's real, and it's effective. No, we cannot overcome these hurdles by ourselves, and kudos to those women who are willing to admit it. So let's call on Him to help and strengthen us. He would love to hear us ask.

Day 92
Closer to Victory

With God we will gain the victory.
PSALM 108:13

God wants us to understand that even though we will experience troubles, we are immune to lasting defeat. Even when we lose, we win because God sees to it that we gain wisdom and understanding from our losses. He reaches out to us with comfort and consolation. Each loss actually brings us closer to victory. Learn from your defeats, and then turn your back on them and reach for God's mercies.

Day 93
A Deeper Understanding

You must have faith and not doubt.
Anyone who doubts is like an ocean
wave tossed around in a storm.

JAMES 1:6 CEV

Bible readers who examine what God says about His eternal love and infinite compassion often stop and ask, "Really?" It's a legitimate question and one God would like to answer. Healthy doubt compels us to ponder His claims and promises. It draws us to pray for God's Spirit to deepen our understanding and sharpen our spiritual vision. Eager inquiry, along with an attentive and receptive mind, guides us from "Really?" to "Wow!"

Day 94

Depression

Be strong and take heart,
all you who hope in the LORD.

PSALM 31:24

For those who live with the darkness of depression, no one has to explain the pain and despair. It's not the kind of thing that can be reasoned away. It's just there, pulling them down, keeping them captive. If you suffer from depression, you should know that God doesn't intend for His children to live in despair. He has an answer for you. Visit your doctor for a check-up, find someone to talk to. When you do what you can, He will be there to do the rest.

Day 95

Promises Fulfilled

What if some did not believe? Will their
unbelief make the faithfulness of God
without effect? Certainly not!

Romans 3:3–4 nkjv

One of the great advantages of studying the Bible is discovering how God, from the beginning of time, has followed through on His promises. Though some of His promises have yet to be fulfilled, why would we doubt them? God does not change, and He has never proved false or unfaithful. We can accept those things in our lives that we don't understand right now, because there's no doubt in God's mind about His love for us.

Day 96

Inside and Out

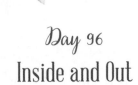

*Why, my soul, are you downcast? Why so
disturbed within me? Put your hope in God,
for I will yet praise him, my Savior and my God.*

PSALM 42:5–6

Depression is often a physiological problem, but just as often it's a result of adverse circumstances. If events in your life have left you in the depths of despair, God wants you to know that you are not alone. He is right there with you. Even when others don't understand, He does. Others only see who you are on the outside, but He knows all about you, inside and out. He knows how to comfort you. Reach out to Him and He will reach back.

Day 97
Extraordinary Love

I weep with sorrow;
encourage me by your word.
PSALM 119:28 NLT

Emotions can whip a woman from laughter to tears and back again in the space of an hour! While violent mood swings may indicate a need for compassionate medical attention, we can embrace our emotions by remembering they are part of the body and spirit our God has created for our good. Used rightly, emotions enable us to feel empathy, express care and concern, and reach out to others with the warmth and humanity of God's extraordinary love.

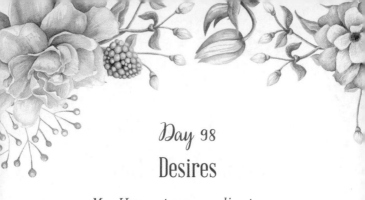

Day 98
Desires

May He grant you according to your
heart's desire, and fulfill all your purpose.

PSALM 20:4 NKJV

What is it you want with all your heart—true love, a great job, children? Only you know what it is. You needn't hold back. Because you are His child, He longs to give you the things that would make you happy. There are some conditions though. Like any good parent, He balances what you want with what He knows is good for you. He isn't interested in your temporary, superficial happiness. He wants to give you more than you ever imagined.

Day 99

His Continued Presence

I am with you always,
even unto the end of the world.

MATTHEW 28:20 KJV

As women, we know our moods change! That's why God, who never changes, warns us against relying on our emotions to discern matters of faith. Instead, He invites us to let His unchanging care, compassion, and love for us assure us of His continued presence, even when emotions tug at us from all directions. His heart hears us, His hands steady us, and His strength supports us on the heights and in the depths of human emotion.

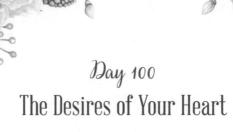

Day 100

The Desires of Your Heart

Take delight in the LORD, and he
will give you the desires of your heart.

PSALM 37:4

As you get to know God better, as you bask in His love
and care, your desires will change. Selfishness and
unwholesome desires will fade away. You will begin
to understand and desire those things He desires for
you—those things that will resonate in your heart and
bring you true happiness. God created you, and He
knows you better than you know yourself. Trust Him
to give you the desires of your heart.

Day 101

His Sweet Presence

Your God, the LORD himself, will be with you.
He will not fail you or abandon you.

DEUTERONOMY 31:6 GNT

We may be happily walking with God, and then suddenly we feel like we're all alone on the path. Where has He gone? Does He no longer care? It's this kind of faith-testing emptiness that works to strengthen our resolve as we continue to seek and to pray, to listen for His voice and grow in His wisdom. At the right time, His sweet presence will flood our spirits with the awesome joy of knowing He has been with us all along!

Day 102

Determination

"Be strong and do not give up,
for your work will be rewarded."

2 Chronicles 15:7

Have you ever watched a marathon? They can be pretty boring until the runners get to the final few miles. Some are so exhausted that they can barely stay on their feet. You want to scream "Give it up! It's just a race!" but they don't give up. The runners are determined to finish. They understand the reward that awaits them on the other side of the finish line, so they keep pushing. That's the kind of determination it takes to please God.

Day 103

He's in Control

Just as we have a share in Christ's many sufferings,
so also through Christ we share in God's great help.

2 Corinthians 1:5 GNT

When someone we love is no longer in our lives, we're left with a painful hole in the center of our hearts. How we wish things had worked out differently! God desires to fill our emptiness with His comfort, understanding, and love. Despite what happened, God remains in control, and His care for us will never waver. Yes, we hurt right now. That's why He's waiting with open arms to embrace us and comfort our sorrowful souls.

Day 104

Rewards Await

Let us hold fast the confession
of our hope without wavering,
for He who promised is faithful.

HEBREWS 10:23 NKJV

God doesn't want you to ever give up on becoming the person He created you to be. He wants to see you follow the dream He's placed in your heart, develop your talent, fulfill your mission in life. Sure, sometimes you will feel like giving up, trying something easier. But remember that a reward waits for you on the other side of the finish line—a reward more wonderful than you can imagine. You can count on that because God has promised.

Day 105

Protected

*Your enemy the devil prowls around like a
roaring lion looking for someone to devour.
Resist him, standing firm in the faith.*

1 PETER 5:8–9

Your strongest and most subtle enemies are not those
you can see but those invisible to the eye. Enemies
like temptation, discouragement, ungodly desires, and
selfishness work to lure you away from God's path and
your trust in Him. Yet through your faith in Jesus Christ,
you walk protected with the shield of God's strength
and power, and you rest secure in knowing God has
overcome all the enemies of love and peace, purity
and joy.

Day 106
Discipleship

Jesus said, "If you hold to my teaching,
you are really my disciples. Then you will
know the truth, and the truth will set you free."

JOHN 8:31–32

Sometimes trying to follow the teachings of Jesus makes you feel as if you're going two steps forward and one step back. The "step back" shouldn't leave you discouraged, however. Instead, let it encourage you to turn to God with a humble heart. He promises to send His Holy Spirit to fill you with strength, confidence, and perseverance as you step forward again in His footsteps.

Day 107

Bridges between Hearts

The righteous cry out, and the LORD hears them;
he delivers them from all their troubles.

PSALM 34:17

Estrangement happens in families and between friends. Where once there had been affection, now there is distance; and though reconciliation seems far off, we continue to love, pray, and hope. We reach out to God, and He graciously fills the empty spot in our hearts. Surrendering all to Him, we find peace in the quiet and courageous work of remaining open and understanding, compassionate and forgiving, for from these things God builds bridges from one heart to another.

Day 108
Genuine Fellowship

[Jesus said,] "A new command I give you:
Love one another. As I have loved you, so you
must love one another. By this everyone will know
that you are my disciples, if you love one another."

JOHN 13:34–35

"He's hard to love." "She's not a lovable person." Whose name comes to mind? This is the very person Jesus invites you to love the same way He loves you—with a heart open to forgiveness, kindness, and compassion. As you follow in Jesus' footsteps, let the Holy Spirit replace your feelings of dislike, anger, or resentment with a disciple's willingness to reach out in genuine fellowship and Christian love.

Day 109
Welcome Back!

Draw near to God,
and he will draw near to you.
JAMES 4:8 NRSV

When God feels the pain of estrangement, it's not because He has strayed from us, but because we have strayed from Him. But no matter why we left or where we've gone, there's one thing we know for sure: We're welcome back. Always. God stands waiting with open arms to receive any wandering soul. He is willing to forgive, eager to celebrate our homecoming, and ready to pour out on us the renewal and refreshment of His lasting peace.

Day 110

Doubts

What if some were unfaithful?
Will their unfaithfulness nullify
God's faithfulness? Not at all!

ROMANS 3:3–4

When you doubt God's power and ability, you then place your trust in someone or something else. Sooner or later, you're sadly disappointed, because no one is capable of meeting your spiritual needs, and no thing or activity on earth can meet your deep longing for fulfillment. Only God can! Throw doubt aside and come back to Him. No matter how long you have been gone, He has been faithful to you and will be there for you.

Day 111
Life!

*"Those who believe in
the Son have eternal life."*
John 3:36 ncv

If we have never visited a place but want to know what it's like, we ask someone who's been there. Jesus, who came from heaven, is the only one who can tell us what heaven is like; and Jesus, who rose from the grave and ascended to heaven, is the only one who can take us there. With our hope and our hearts resting in His hands, we have nothing to fear, not even death. Why? Because, in Him, death means life—eternal life.

Day 112

Unwavering Love

*[Jesus] said to them, "Why are you troubled,
and why do doubts rise in your minds?"*

LUKE 24:38

God never condemns you for doubting. Instead, He invites you to use doubt as a springboard to find out more about Him, His love for you, and His plan for you to live with Him in heaven. Give voice to your doubts, looking to Him for answers through Bible study, meditation, and the counsel of mature Christians. Let your doubts work to take you toward a greater appreciation of your God and His unwavering love for you.

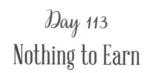

Day 113

Nothing to Earn

*God's gift is eternal life given
by Jesus Christ our Lord.*

Romans 6:23 cev

If God required you to earn eternal life, you'd have every reason to worry! After all, how would you know when, or if, you've done enough? That's why God brings eternal life to you through Jesus. Jesus' sin-free life means you have nothing to earn, but only to receive, as He offers to you the perfection He already has won. He has provided a way for you to have eternal life, and the way is nothing other than Himself.

Day 114
Dreams

*For God is working in you, giving you the
desire and the power to do what pleases him.*

PHILIPPIANS 2:13 NLT

When "no" evicts your cherished hopes and dreams,
bitterness often moves in—and stays. Avoid the temptation to let disappointment replace your dreams, and
instead let God's Spirit find a home in your heart. Tell
Him your dreams then listen for His answer. Discover
His "yes" in the blessings around you, in your abilities
and opportunities, and in the work He has given you
to do. Let following Him be your dream come true!

Day 115
Ultimate Trust

*Because of the LORD's great love we are
not consumed, for his compassions never fail.*

LAMENTATIONS 3:22

Despite the anguish failure leaves behind, there's something positive to take away. Amid the frequent failure of families to prosper, of health to improve, of money to bring security, and of relationships to last, God once again reminds us that our ultimate trust belongs in Him. Nothing else but His presence has a guarantee attached to it, and no earthly person or thing can promise us spiritual peace without fail. But God can, and He does.

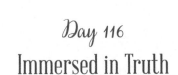

Day 116

Immersed in Truth

Who hopes for what they already have?
But if we hope for what we do not
yet have, we wait for it patiently.

ROMANS 8:24–25

God has no desire for you to be misled by lies that masquerade as truth. While popular myths and wishful thinking sometimes offer feel-good solutions, God has given you His Word so you can know the difference between dreams and reality. He invites you to immerse yourself, not in wishful thinking that evaporates in a day, but in sound teachings that will lead you to the truth and remain with you throughout eternity.

Day 117
God-Given Vision

Never let go of loyalty and faithfulness.
PROVERBS 3:3 GNT

Dedicated inventors and innovators are those who remain faithful to their idea, despite years, or even a lifetime, of scorn. In a similar way, our faithfulness to God's commandments and His will often attracts ridicule, because not everyone looks at life with spiritual eyes and sees what we see. Our God-given vision of forgiveness and compassion, dignity and justice, understanding and love for everyone keeps us working faithfully to make His idea for the world a reality.

Day 118
Duty

Whatever work you do, do your best.

ECCLESIASTES 9:10 NCV

By necessity, many people work in jobs they don't like or feel suited for. For them, work is a duty rather than a dream. If you find yourself in that situation, there is something you can do. Take one day at a time and focus your attention on your responsibilities for that day. Give it your all as a token of your love and respect for God. You will either begin to see your job differently, or God will find you a new assignment. He always rewards the diligent.

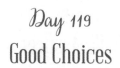

Day 119
Good Choices

The Lord is faithful, and he will strengthen
you and keep you safe from the Evil One.

2 Thessalonians 3:3 gnt

When the choice before us is going along with others or remaining true to what we believe is right, we know which choice to make. But knowing isn't enough! God's Spirit working within us gives us the strength and conviction it takes to remain faithful to ourselves and our loved ones, to our promises, our ideals, and our responsibilities. When acting on our good choices takes courage, we can rest at ease in His faithfulness to us.

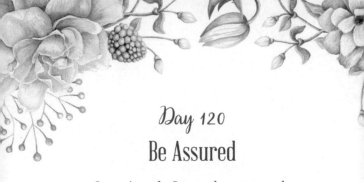

Day 120

Be Assured

Commit to the LORD whatever you do,
and he will establish your plans.

PROVERBS 16:3

God is never without a plan, and He has one for your life as well. There will be times when you wonder how your current job could be part of that plan. Maybe you are just spinning your wheels, doing your duty. Be assured that God has a purpose for everything you put your hand to. Perhaps it's a lesson you need to learn or a skill you will one day need. Begin to look at your job in the context of God's wisdom and you'll see His hand in all you do.

Day 121
From God

A wise woman strengthens her family.

PROVERBS 14:1 NCV

It's likely that the place we exert the most influence is right in our own family. Our day-to-day decisions, conduct, and attitude affect the lives of those closest to us in ways that may span generations. When the source of our strength and wisdom comes from God, we are like the woman who showers life-giving water on tender flowers. As they grow, beauty and sweetness surround us, and goodness and kindness flow back to us.

Day 122
Emotion

Weeping may stay for the night,
but rejoicing comes in the morning.

PSALM 30:5

When your emotions leave you sitting at the bottom of a dark pit, it's hard to believe in daylight. That's why the Bible speaks so clearly on the fleeting nature of human feelings and the eternal nature of God's presence and His love. He sends you dawn after night, spring after winter, joy after sorrow, to remind you that even in the depths of sorrow, there is the height—and the light—of His love.

Day 123
The Abundant Life

"Fear not, for I am with you; be not dismayed, for I am your God. I will strengthen you, yes, I will help you."

Isaiah 41:10 NKJV

Fear, as unsettling as it is, can signal danger and deter us from taking ill-advised risks. But it can also drain our energy, turn us inward, and hinder us from enjoying the abundant life God has in mind for us. He can show us how to separate healthy and justified fear from unnecessary dread that burdens our hearts and spirits. Lay destructive fears on His shoulders, and let Him surround you with His strength, courage, and confidence.

Day 124
Always Listening

The Lord hath heard the voice of my weeping.
The Lord hath heard my supplication;
the Lord will receive my prayer.

PSALM 6:8–9 KJV

God has not abandoned you in your weeping. Neither does He judge you for your feelings, nor does He offer you a useless platitude in response to your sorrow. Instead, He comforts you by opening His arms to you, inviting you to talk to Him about your feelings and the depth of your emotions. Even more, He promises He will listen. Go to Him in confidence, even if you're not sure what to say. He is listening to you.

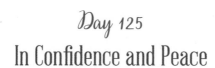

Day 125

In Confidence and Peace

"Do not fear or be dismayed; tomorrow go out against them, and the LORD will be with you."

2 CHRONICLES 20:17 NRSV

Sometimes fear is all that's standing between us and what we long to do. We get butterflies in our stomachs when we encounter new people, interview for a job, or ask for a raise in pay. When fear blocks our way ahead, we can let God take His place in front of us, beside us, and behind us. As He opens the way, we can move forward in confidence and peace.

Day 126

Emptiness

*It was not with perishable things such as silver or
gold that you were redeemed from the empty way
of life handed down to you from your ancestors,
but with the precious blood of Christ,
a lamb without blemish or defect.*

1 PETER 1:18–19

A deep feeling of emptiness drives many to addiction,
despair, and risky behavior. Without a sense of meaning
and purpose in their lives, who could blame them?
Maybe you find yourself in that very place—empty
through and through—but you don't have to live that
way. God loves you and He has a purpose and plan
for your life—a plan that will challenge you and bring
you joy and fulfillment. Let Him fill you with His Holy
Spirit and show you who you were created to be.

Day 127
The Command to Forgive

Put up with each other, and forgive anyone who does you wrong, just as Christ has forgiven you.

COLOSSIANS 3:13 CEV

In the Bible, God doesn't simply suggest we forgive others; He commands it! Why? Because without it, there's no room for authentic peace. When we forgive the offenses others commit against us, we're acknowledging that we too have sinned and stand in need of forgiveness. It's through genuinely forgiving others and humbly accepting forgiveness from others and from God that we come to experience true peace of mind and heart.

Day 128
Endurance

*Let us run with endurance the race that
is set before us, looking unto Jesus,
the author and finisher of our faith.*

HEBREWS 12:1–2 NKJV

You long to scream "enough!" and turn your back on everything, but you don't. At times like this, God raises your spiritual eyes to Jesus, the one who not only walks with you, but who has gone before you to the end. Trust Him to take you to the finish. There you will thank Him for making it possible for you to endure present hardship and reap the eternal reward of achieving His purpose for your life.

Day 129
Scattered Darkness

I forgive you all that you have done,
says the Lord GOD.

EZEKIEL 16:63 NRSV

Deep within many of our hearts lies a sin we're ashamed of. We're so ashamed that we don't want anyone else to know about it, least of all God! Yet when we realize God already sees the inmost part of our hearts and yearns to shine His light of love, compassion, and forgiveness there, we're compelled to confess what has burdened us for so long. Only God can scatter the darkness and set our troubled hearts at rest.

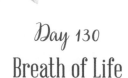

Day 130
Breath of Life

I pray that you, being rooted and established in love, may have power, together with all the Lord's holy people, to grasp how wide and long and high and deep is the love of Christ, and to know this love that surpasses knowledge–that you may be filled to the measure of all the fullness of God.

EPHESIANS 3:17–19

Empty calories lurk in foods of no nutritional value. Similarly, empty emotions are hidden in foolish thoughts, selfish pursuits, and meaningless activities. They leave you unfulfilled, never satisfying your real needs. God's love isn't like that—it's deep, refreshing, renewing, restoring, and loaded with spiritual nutrients. Breathe it in! Swallow it! Fill yourself with its strength and power, and you will never feel empty again.

Day 131
Eternal Friendship

[Jesus said,] "I have called you friends."
JOHN 15:15 NKJV

A friend is someone we can confide in, who's there for us, who cares and understands. All that and more is the kind of friend God wants to be to us. More than even our closest longtime friends, God knows where we came from, the children we used to be, and the women we are now—and He loves us through and through. His is a friendship available to us today and one that will carry us into eternity.

Day 132
Deep Truth

When your endurance is fully developed,
you will be perfect and complete, needing nothing.
JAMES 1:4 NLT

How easy it would be to give up! And the truth is, many people would. Yet deep in your heart you know God asks you to carry on until you receive God-given release. Why? Because He has full spiritual maturity in mind for you. You may be unable to figure out how your current situation can lead you to a fuller, more joyful tomorrow, but God knows. Put your trust in Him as you continue on the way He has laid out for you.

Day 133

Bringing Hearts Together

*One who forgives an
affront fosters friendship.*

PROVERBS 17:9 NRSV

Many things can come between friends: anger, jealousy,
hurt, or blame. When friends stubbornly refuse to extend
their hands in forgiveness, the rift can go on for years,
if not a lifetime. If there's a place in our hearts only a
certain friend could fill, perhaps in her heart there's an
empty spot where we used to be. God knows both, and
He knows how to bring hearts together in forgiveness,
kindness, and peace.

Day 134
Envy

Love is patient, love is kind. It does not envy,
it does not boast, it is not proud.

1 Corinthians 13:4

When envy fills the heart, there's no room left for love. If you have been sidetracked by envy, ask God to help you regain your thoughts and emotions by forgiving you and putting you back on the right path. Once the Lord sweeps your heart clean, you will have a dwelling place fit for humility, kindliness, compassion, and love.

Day 135
A Better Way

"I know the plans I have for you," declares the LORD,
"plans to prosper you and not to harm you,
plans to give you hope and a future."

JEREMIAH 29:11

The future is loaded with uncertainty. Some of us react by feeling powerless to make any change in our circumstances, and others by growing bitter when the years fail to unfold according to our plans. God has a better way. He invites us to know that He is in control and to put our future into His hands. He encourages us to pray and work today, and accept with gratitude all He has in store for us tomorrow.

Day 136

Eternal Joy

Don't for a minute envy careless rebels;
soak yourself in the Fear-of-God—
That's where your future lies. Then you
won't be left with an armload of nothing.

PROVERBS 23:17 MSG

You see people living in carefree disregard of God's "thou shalt nots." When they appear so lighthearted and happy, it's hard to not envy them. But you should not. Their lives are headed nowhere. Turn your admiring glance instead to God's Word and read His promises for those who walk rightly. There is great comfort in knowing that following Him will bring you a lifetime—and eternity—of joy.

Day 137

A Better Tomorrow

*What you ought to say is, "If the Lord wants
us to, we will live and do this or that."*

JAMES 4:15 NLT

When we were young, most of us lunged into the future
with energy and optimism. Then, as years passed, we
found that some of our plans worked out and some did
not. Focusing on today's good helps us plan better for
tomorrow. And although we now step ahead with perhaps a little less vitality and a more balanced perspective,
we have found that the future leads nowhere unless God
is guiding and we are following His way.

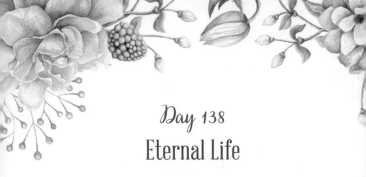

Day 138
Eternal Life

[Jesus said,] "Very truly I tell you the truth,
whoever hears my word and believes him who
sent me has eternal life and will not be judged;
but has crossed over from death to life."

JOHN 5:24

When you're tempted to live for the moment, consider this: God has given you eternal life right now. God means for you to give up a human, short-sighted perspective and live as if you're living for eternity—because you are. Ask God to allow His Spirit to stretch your spiritual sight beyond this moment. Let Him show you what matters for all eternity; then commit yourself to live in it.

Day 139
Delights

You must each decide in your heart how much to give.
And don't give reluctantly or in response to pressure.
"For God loves a person who gives cheerfully."

2 Corinthians 9:7 NLT

When we count our blessings, do we ever ask ourselves why God gave them to us in the first place? Sure, He blesses us with everything we need for our well-being, and also with what He delights to give us for our comfort and enjoyment. He blesses us too so we can delight in sharing our time, abilities, talents, and financial resources with others. In God's world, "blessing" and "sharing" and "happiness" travel together.

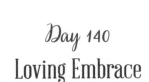

Day 140

Loving Embrace

[Jesus said,] "God so loved the world that he gave his one and only Son, that whoever believes in him shall not perish but have eternal life."

JOHN 3:16

"Why would almighty God love me?" you ask. "And why would He open heaven to me when I've done nothing to deserve it?" Yes, God's unconditional love is beyond human understanding, but it's there for you. His plan of salvation is all about taking who you are and making you who you were created to be. No matter how strongly you may feel you don't deserve God, embrace Him as firmly and as tenderly as He embraces you.

Day 141
True Riches

The generous will prosper; those who refresh others will themselves be refreshed.

PROVERBS 11:25 NLT

True riches come not from gathering as much as possible, but from giving as much as possible. Think of the warm feeling we get when we are able to help someone in need, or when we give of our time and effort to make a positive difference for others. This is the only wealth guaranteed to grow in value and the only riches certain to last a lifetime—and beyond. The more we give, the more we receive.

Day 142

Example

To this you were called, because Christ
suffered for you, leaving you an example,
that you should follow in his steps.

1 PETER 2:21

Even Jesus' closest disciples—men and women who traveled with Him during His earthly ministry—did not always follow His example. At times they bickered among themselves, doubted His words, misunderstood His ministry, and denied they even knew Him. Nonetheless, Jesus' healing forgiveness was there for them, just as it is for you. Ask Him and He will teach you how to walk in His footsteps.

Day 143

Celebration

Our only goal is to please God.

2 CORINTHIANS 5:9 NCV

When we're working toward a goal, we look forward to celebrating as soon as we reach it. But our time between now and then is something to celebrate too. The process of planning and creating of learning and building, is often more thrilling than achieving what we had set out to do. Yes, let's keep our eyes on the goal, but keep our hearts and minds on the miracle of every moment that we spend getting there.

Day 144
Perfect Love

*Be an example to the believers in word,
in conduct, in love, in spirit, in faith, in purity.*

1 TIMOTHY 4:12 NKJV

When you consider how many people you influence every day through your words, attitude, and actions, you realize how often you set a less-than-stellar example. God uses these times to impress on you how much He wants you to make Him a vital part of your life—not just when it's easy but every day, every hour, every minute. Let your entire life become an example of His love for you.

Day 145

Proceed in Peace

May He grant you according to your heart's desire,
and fulfill all your purpose.

PSALM 20:4 NKJV

Sometimes when we set an objective for ourselves, we experience a time of insecurity. Can we really pull it off? At those times, it's good to talk to God about it. Better than we do, He knows our strengths and abilities and what we're capable of achieving. After all, He gave us the physical, intellectual, creative, and spiritual resources we possess. If we lay out our goals before Him, asking Him for His blessing and His help, we will feel much more confident throughout the process. Then we can proceed in peace.

Day 146

Expectation

In the morning, LORD, you hear my voice;
in the morning I lay my requests
before you and wait expectantly.

PSALM 5:3

You have taken your heartfelt requests to God, and now you are waiting for His response. Don't grow impatient. Instead, relish this time of hopeful expectation. Rehearse the ways God has come through for you in the past. Allow thanksgiving to flow freely from your lips. Like a child on the day before her birthday, enjoy a confident excitement concerning what God is going to do on your behalf. He is a gracious Father who can be trusted without hesitation.

Day 147

Belonging to Him

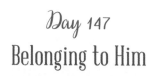

The fear of the LORD is
the beginning of knowledge.
PROVERBS 1:7 NKJV

Does the thought of God, with power and authority over all things, make us tremble? If so, it means we sense the reality of His existence and the extent of His might—after all, it's that might that protects us and brings us the help we need in troubled times. He is also the God who offers us unconditional love, overwhelming compassion, and gracious plans for our lives. Isn't it wonderful to serve an all-powerful God who invites us to belong to Him and live as His beloved daughters now and forever?

Day 148

Strength and Comfort

My soul, wait silently for God alone,
for my expectation is from Him.

PSALM 62:5 NKJV

Sometimes people fail to live up to your expectations, and sometimes you fail to live up to the values and standards you have for yourself. As you take your hurt, your embarrassment, your shame to God, don't forget His unchangeable love for you. He has promised you the gift of His Holy Spirit to give you strength and comfort, and you should expect no less. He will never fail you.

Day 149

Loving Who God Is

"Let us acknowledge the LORD;
let us press on to acknowledge him."

HOSEA 6:3

Those of us who have ever betrayed our true selves to please someone else know we made a big mistake. That's why God remains God rather than conforming to our notions about Him, or about what He should do for us. In the Bible, God reveals His unconditional love for us, and in creation He displays His creative power. Peace with God comes not from asking Him to be what He isn't, but by loving who He is.

Day 150

Experience

We know that in all things God works for
the good of those who love him, who have
been called according to his purpose.

ROMANS 8:28

Perhaps God is permitting you to undergo an unhappy or hurtful experience, and you understandably wonder why. How can He stand by and let you suffer? While the reason why may remain unanswered this side of heaven, His care for you and involvement in your life is a given. He will use this experience to draw you closer to Him, and in it He will bring about good.

Day 151
His Good Will

The world and its desire are passing away,
but those who do the will of God live forever.

1 JOHN 2:17 NRSV

Peace is impossible when our human wills collide with God's will. Yet unlike a person who insists on imposing her own will for selfish reasons, God makes His will known to us for our benefit. He recognizes where our talents lie and where our happiness rests. He sees beyond the present moment and has determined the best path for our feet. He never forces His desires on us, but delights to lead us where His good and gracious will would take us.

Day 152

His Own

You will show me the way of life,
granting me the joy of your presence
and the pleasures of living with you forever.

PSALM 16:11 NLT

How long has it been since you have allowed yourself to experience the spiritual joys of life? Don't let the day's troubles, a busy schedule, and other distractions strip you of the everyday pleasures God has set before you. Consider the fact He has called you to be His own. Meditate on His presence in your life and what it means to you. Give thanks today for the blessings of the day and experience His love for you!

Day 153
Always

*"Stand at the crossroads and look; ask for
the ancient paths, ask where the good way is,
and walk in it, and you will find rest for your souls."*

JEREMIAH 6:16

God's will for us is not always perfectly clear. We can imagine Him asking us to stick with Him a little longer, and perhaps discover His answer for ourselves as time passes. Sometimes His answers come in the unfolding of events, in the "chance" encounter with a wise and insightful friend, or in the words of scripture as we study more deeply and pray more fervently. God's will is always for us to walk more closely with Him.

Day 154
Failure

If we are unfaithful, he remains faithful,
for he cannot deny who he is.

2 TIMOTHY 2:13 NLT

You have fallen down, and now what? God is waiting to pick you up again, to dust you off, to comfort and strengthen you so you can go on. Even if you've fallen because you strayed from God's commandments, His strong arms still wait for you. All you need do is call out to Him and ask Him to help you get back on your feet again. God is waiting. Reach up to Him!

Day 155

Abundance

I will thank the LORD
with all my heart.

PSALM 111:1 NCV

Gratitude creates peace, and peace creates gratitude. When we take time out to give thanks for the blessings that we enjoy each day, we realize how much God has given us. And if He has blessed us today, we can trust Him to bless us tomorrow as well. Reliance on Him produces serenity of heart and mind, giving us all the more reason to thank Him again for the abundance of peace we have in Him!

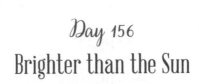

Day 156

Brighter than the Sun

Everyone born of God overcomes the world.
This is the victory that has overcome
the world, even our faith.

1 JOHN 5:4

You are living your faith, but to some people you're a failure. You fail to measure success by the world's standards, and you fail to go along with popular thinking and adopt ungodly values as your own. Let your soul be glad when people call you a failure, because it proves your faith is evident to others. In God's eyes, you have conquered the world. You have rich fellowship with Him and a future brighter than the sun.

Day 157
Plenty of Good

Be thankful in all circumstances.

1 Thessalonians 5:18 nlt

It's easy to forget gratitude when face-to-face with trouble, yet gratitude offers unfailing support and help. Gratitude gives us perspective by showing us that, despite the bad, there's still plenty of good around us. It saves us from despair by assuring us that all is not lost, and it instills in us strength to determine our best response and take hold of a productive solution to our problems. A grateful heart is a faithful friend in time of need.

Day 158
Family Life

Bear with each other and forgive one another
if any of you has a grievance against someone.
Forgive as the Lord forgave you. And over
all these virtues put on love, which binds
them all together in perfect unity.

COLOSSIANS 3:13–14

No family is perfect, and nearly everyone will at some-time hurt, betray, and disappoint a family member. In extreme cases it may be necessary to distance yourself. But in all cases, it is necessary to forgive. Let God judge the person or people who caused the pain. To you He says, "Forgive." When you do, you will no longer harm yourself with the corrosive emotions of anger and resentment. Instead, you will become more like Christ, who long ago forgave you.

Day 159

His Healing Heart

I want you to understand what really matters,
so that you may live pure and blameless
lives until the day of Christ's return.

PHILIPPIANS 1:10 NLT

For various reasons, we often accept as fact the accusations of others, and we feel responsible for the way they feel. But God does not hold us accountable for the choices others make, only for our own. When our guilt is justified, He is eager to hear our confession and lift its burden from us. When guilt does not belong to us, God strengthens us and helps us lead a hurting soul to His healing heart.

Day 160

Living in Harmony

Live in harmony with one another.

ROMANS 12:16

Why all the arguments, the bitterness, the ugly words? In your home, everyone feels tense and defensive, and you know this is not what God intends for your family. Let Him put things right, beginning with you. Ask His Spirit to show you how to live in godly harmony with all the members of your family. Let Him teach you the words and actions that create genuine affection and lasting unity. Let God's peace begin with you and comfort everyone with His presence.

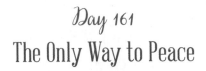

Day 161
The Only Way to Peace

*"I have swept away your offenses like
a cloud, your sins like the morning mist.
Return to me, for I have redeemed you."*

ISAIAH 44:22

When we have done wrong, guilt keeps our transgression in front of us. Justifiable guilt is the tool God uses to draw us toward Him and the confession of our sin. He yearns to renew our minds and hearts by assuring us of His forgiveness. God longs to restore the bond sin severs between individuals, and between Himself and us. Forgiveness, the only way to peace, begins with a simple, sincere prayer of acknowledgment that, yes, we have sinned.

Day 162
Faults

Confess your faults one to another,
and pray one for another, that ye may be healed.
JAMES 5:16 KJV

Criticism hurts. While your first reaction is, quite naturally, to retaliate, God has an alternative in mind. Listen to the words of your critic, He says. If your critic has pinpointed a fault in your conduct or character, give thanks you have someone in your life who is frank and truthful enough to tell you where you need to make changes. Ask the Holy Spirit to help you mature and grow in this area.

Day 163

His Spirit

Happy are those to whom the LORD imputes no iniquity, and in whose spirit there is no deceit.

PSALM 32:2 NRSV

Like a pan of simmering water, dishonesty never rests. It keeps us on edge, fearing someone will reveal our deception, our duplicity. God would have us come to Him so He can bathe us in the still, cool waters of His forgiveness. Then, He invites us to allow His Spirit into our hearts. Through His Spirit, we possess the strength, confidence, and courage to live our lives with honesty and integrity.

Day 164
A Vibrant Follower

*All Scripture is inspired by God and is useful
for teaching, for showing people what is
wrong in their lives, for correcting faults,
and for teaching how to live right.*

2 TIMOTHY 3:16 NCV

If you feel uncomfortable when you read God's commandments and hear His guidelines for your life, good! The discomfort you feel when facing your faults means the Holy Spirit is at work in you, molding you more and more into a living, breathing, active, vibrant follower of Jesus Christ. Welcome your discomfort. Pray about the faults God's Word points out, and learn what you need to do to overcome them.

Day 165

Authenticity

[Jesus said,] "Whoever can be trusted with very little can also be trusted with much, and whoever is dishonest with very little will also be dishonest with much."

LUKE 16:10

Being dishonest, even in trivial matters, is like wearing a mask. It hides who we really are and invites others to believe a lie. It even enables us to deceive ourselves. Yet God is never deceived, and He has no desire for us to be deceived by anyone. Whenever dishonesty creeps into our thinking, actions, or relationships, we can turn to Him for the courage and confidence to turn our authentic face to the world.

Day 166
Fear

I will fear no evil, for you are with me;
your rod and your staff, they comfort me.

PSALM 23:4

Do you find yourself trembling when television newscasters predict hard times ahead? Could things really get as bad as they say? Take heart! God reaches out to you, as He has to His people throughout history, and offers His comfort in a world full of uncomfortable news and troublesome events. No matter what happens or doesn't happen, your all-powerful and all-knowing God is your strength and salvation. You can rest at ease in Him.

Day 167

In the Right Place

The Lord is good to those who hope
in him, to those who seek him.

LAMENTATIONS 3:25 NCV

Sometimes we reach the sad realization that we have put our hope in the wrong place. During such times, we appreciate even more the hope God extends to us through the life, death, and resurrection of Jesus. Through His Son, God demonstrated His desire to heal us, forgive us, renew us, and grant us eternal life with Him in heaven. When we put our hope in Him, our hope is in the right place now and forever.

Day 168

Forgiven and Beloved

"Do not fear, for I have redeemed you; I have summoned you by name; you are mine."

ISAIAH 43:1

In a world of more than seven billion souls, fear of becoming "just a number" ranks high among modern-day stressors. God removes the reason for your nagging fear of anonymity when He says to you, "I know your name" and "You are Mine." He loves you personally, and He claims you personally. In Jesus Christ, you possess an eternal identity as a forgiven and beloved child of God.

Day 169

Hope of Heaven

Things that are seen don't last forever,
but things that are not seen are eternal.
That's why we keep our minds on the
things that cannot be seen.

2 Corinthians 4:18 cev

You may say, "I hope so!" when the outcome is iffy. Yet the hope God holds out for us is strengthened with His truth and secured with His promises. There's nothing iffy about it! Our hope of heaven, though not yet apparent to our physical eyes, is sure because God is faithful and does what He says He will do. We may not know all the particulars, but we don't need to when our hope rests in Him.

Day 170

Forgiveness

You are a forgiving God,
gracious and compassionate,
slow to anger and abounding in love.

NEHEMIAH 9:17

Perhaps the sin was huge, and you're still suffering its consequences. Even though you feel deeply sorry for what you did and have apologized to those you hurt, guilt burdens your heart and weighs your spirit. Do not let that sin continue on its damaging rampage through your soul. Instead, give your sorrow to the God who is bigger than any sin you could possibly commit. Be comforted by His promise of restoration and renewal, and go forward in forgiveness.

Day 171
Humble Hearts

*Good and upright is the LORD; therefore he instructs
sinners in the way. He leads the humble in what
is right, and teaches the humble his way.*

PSALM 25:8–9 NRSV

The humility God desires stems from a heart flowing
with His love for people. God sent His Son—who died
and rose again to show us His love—to bring every soul
to Himself, something not one of us could do on our
own. Although we have no cause to boast, we do have
every reason to see ourselves as beloved daughters of
God, of infinite worth in our heavenly Father's sight. As
such, our humble hearts look to Him and give thanks!

Day 172

Humble Courage

Make allowance for each other's faults,
and forgive anyone who offends you. Remember,
the Lord forgave you, so you must forgive others.

COLOSSIANS 3:13 NLT

No one wants to be the first to say "I'm sorry." No one jumps to take responsibility for a misspoken word, a hurtful act, a mismanaged situation. But without someone possessing the humble courage to extend the hand of peace, no healing can ever take place. Do your part by stepping forward, admitting your part, and asking forgiveness of anyone you may have offended. Jesus forgave you first. True heart healing begins with your willingness to be first in the same way.

Day 173
Gift of Humility

Humble yourselves before the Lord,
and he will lift you up.

JAMES 4:10 GNT

Humility never asks us to deny our accomplishments or run from earned praise. Rather, it simply invites us to remember from whom our gifts, talents, intellect, achievements, and opportunities come. It leads us to feel good when God uses us to inspire and motivate others and when our work makes a difference in the world. A heart blessed with the gift of humility is as close as a prayer, freely available to everyone who asks.

Day 174

Freedom

The LORD sets prisoners free.

PSALM 146:7

We take for granted the ability to move about at will, make independent choices, and manage our own affairs. Many in this world are not so fortunate. They are prisoners. Some are being held in prison for illegal acts; others live in nations where they are prisoners by the will of the government. Still others are prisoners of their own behaviors and excesses. To all the prisoners, God offers the freedom to receive His love and grace, the freedom to know Him and serve Him. Are you in need of freedom?

Day 175
Rooted in Love

You must be compassionate,
just as your Father is compassionate.
LUKE 6:36 NLT

When infirmity of body, intellect, or spirit strikes a loved one, we're often at a loss, not knowing what to say or do. Yet those who suffer need us the most! When we thoughtfully consider how we would like to be treated under the same circumstances, how to respond to others becomes clear. It's a response rooted in love and compassion, giving us the peace of knowing that we have done the right thing.

Day 176

Lasting Liberty

Where the Spirit of the Lord is,
there is freedom.

2 CORINTHIANS 3:17 NCV

Though some might think of the Christian way as paved with restrictions, just the opposite is true. In the Christian message, God offers you the priceless freedom of living each day free from the chains of guilt, despair, and hopelessness. He has opened to you the door to freedom as His Spirit directs you along the path He has laid out for you—a path leading to genuine happiness and lasting liberty.

Day 177
Visit with Him

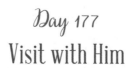

Trust in the LORD with all your heart,
and lean not on your own understanding;
in all your ways acknowledge Him,
and He shall direct your paths.

PROVERBS 3:5–6 NKJV

God cares about the decisions we make, both big and small. He invites us to come to Him when we don't know which way to turn and let Him point us in the right direction. His response may come in the whisper of our intuition, the stirring of our feelings, the conviction of our hearts, or the voice of a wise friend or counselor. Often, our indecision is God's invitation to visit with Him, to tell Him what's on our minds.

Day 178

Friendship

Wounds from a friend can be trusted.
PROVERBS 27:6

It could be that a friend told you the truth, and it hit you hard. Resentment welled up inside you, and you had to bite your tongue not to say anything. Now you wonder if your friendship will ever be the same again. No, it won't be. It will be better. In her, you have a friend who thinks enough of you to share her deepest concerns, no matter how sensitive or difficult the subject. Give thanks to God for the comfort of a true friend.

Day 179

Life Decisions

Whether you turn to the right or to the left,
your ears will hear a voice behind you,
saying, "This is the way; walk in it."

ISAIAH 30:21

A commitment to God's principles turns major life decisions into no-brainers! No, we're not going to think, do, or say what God has forbidden; and yes, we are going to think, do, and say what He has commanded. The opinions of others and even our own feelings fail to upset us, because our Spirit-schooled hearts have already chosen the path they will take. Meanwhile, we can concentrate on life's other choices, like which shoes we'll wear today!

Day 180
Fulfilling Friendship

As iron sharpens iron,
so a friend sharpens a friend.
PROVERBS 27:17 NLT

The angry words really flew between the two of you, and now you wonder if there's anything left of your friendship. When friendship proves challenging, consider how God can use the situation. He may have something to show the two of you about learning from and growing with each other. He may be pushing both of you toward a deeper, more fulfilling friendship—a friendship meant to last a lifetime.

Day 181
Pardon

Love one another deeply from the heart.

1 PETER 1:22 NRSV

Intolerance has two victims: one, the target of mean-spirited thinking and stereotyping; and two, the heart that harbors it. God works to bring peace to both sides: He embraces victims of intolerance with the spirit of forgiveness so they may pardon others as their heavenly Father has forgiven them; and He stirs the feelings of perpetrators so they are led to seek peace with God by loving others with the unconditional, accepting love God has for everyone.

Day 182
Fulfillment

A longing fulfilled is a tree of life.
PROVERBS 13:12

Your deepest longings and cherished dreams hold a special place in your heart, and they hold a special place in God's heart too. He cares what you care about. If you yearn for the fulfillment of your dreams and desires, bring them to the One who knows all about needs, desires, longings, yearnings—and miracles. Trust Him to draw from your dreams the pleasure of godly fulfillment and the satisfaction of true contentment.

Day 183
A Loving Invitation

Love is patient, love is kind.

1 CORINTHIANS 13:4

When we uphold God's moral law, we may be labeled "intolerant" by those who wish to follow their own desires. Yet our godly intolerance is not aimed at individuals, but at behavior God has called wrong and conduct outside His will for people. Our goal is not to judge others (God will take care of that), but to lovingly invite them to reach out to the God of forgiveness, compassion, and love, because His arms are reaching out to them.

Day 184

Beloved Child

I cry out to God Most High,
to God, who vindicates me.

PSALM 57:2

You have looked for fulfillment in many places but have discovered nothing but worthless promises. You are not alone! Throughout the Bible, people just like you have raised empty hands to God, begging Him to soothe the deepest longings of their hearts. He heard their pleas, and He hears yours too. Look to Him. Let His Holy Spirit show you how to find true and lasting fulfillment in living as the beloved child He has created you to be.

Day 185

Contentment

It is better to be content with what little you have.
Otherwise, you will always be struggling for more,
and that is like chasing the wind.

ECCLESIASTES 4:6 NCV

As we more fully embrace God's will for our lives and accept His wisdom in all things concerning us, jealousy becomes less and less of a threat to our inner peace. There's no room in our hearts for envy, because our hearts overflow with gratitude for everything God has given to us. We cannot imagine coveting the life or possessions of another, because we rest content in the privilege of being who we are, beloved daughters of God.

Day 186
Giving

Give freely and spontaneously. Don't have a stingy heart. The way you handle matters like this triggers God, your God's, blessing in everything you do, all your work and ventures.

DEUTERONOMY 15:10 MSG

Fundraisers and donation campaigns ignite guilt feelings. We begrudgingly pledge a small amount, then we add to our guilt the feeling of being manipulated into giving. God wants a whole new attitude. He stands ready to bless the generous giver, the one who gives with a genuinely cheerful heart. Remember, you possess nothing now that God hasn't given you in the first place. Let your giving flow from a heart of gratitude and love.

Day 187
Our Worship

*You must worship no other gods, for the L*ORD*, whose very name is Jealous, is a God who is jealous about his relationship with you.*

EXODUS 34:14 NLT

It's hard to think of God as being jealous, isn't it? He is, and in all the right ways! As our Creator and Lord, God is justifiably jealous of any person or thing we might revere in His place. He knows our security lies in no other name but His, and He sees the destructive path ahead for those who follow false gods. That's why God demands our worship—not because *He* needs it, but because He knows *we* do.

Day 188

Perfect Directions

[Jesus said,] "Give, and it will be given to you. A good measure, pressed down, shaken together and running over, will be poured into your lap. For with the measure you use, it will be measured to you."

LUKE 6:38

If you want more, give more. That's God's way, and He invites you to make it your way too. He promises you abundance when you generously share your time, efforts, resources, and abilities. Do so without expecting a reward, knowing all along God will reward you in far greater measure than you can imagine, in far more directions than you expect. Give His way a try, and find out for yourself.

Day 189
Our Eternal Leader

[Jesus said,] "Whoever wants to be a leader among you must be your servant."
MATTHEW 20:26 NLT

Whether we have looked forward to a leadership position, or it was thrust upon us, we now bear its many responsibilities. But as long as we follow God, our eternal leader, our headship will serve to bless those under our direction. His leadership shields us from the pitfalls of pride and the misuse of power. His way opens our hearts to forgive those who may criticize us unfairly, and embraces us with His wisdom, strength, and confidence.

Day 190
Grace

*How rich is God's grace, which he
has given to us so fully and freely.*
EPHESIANS 1:7–8 NCV

You may be having a difficult time accepting God's undeserved love. Instead, you expect to pay for what you buy and work for what you earn. When it comes to His undeserved love—His grace—you bring the same thinking with you. God's grace, however, works differently. His grace is yours, and it isn't possible to pay for it, earn it, or deserve it. God's grace is yours, not because of you, but because of God.

Day 191
Spiritual Leaders

Be an example to all believers in what you say, in the way you live, in your love, your faith, and your purity.

1 TIMOTHY 4:12 NLT

As women who follow God, we are spiritual leaders. God, through the work of the Holy Spirit evident in the things we do and say, gives us the privilege of guiding others to Him by our example. Our willingness to forgive leads others in the way of forgiveness, and our genuine happiness, true contentment, and inner peace influence others more than we'll ever know. More than ever, we must follow God, and lead with genuine joy!

Day 192
All-Embracing

Out of his fullness we have all received
grace in place of grace already given.

JOHN 1:16

Have you ever shown kindness to someone "just because"? God works in a similar way. He is kind, gracious, and generous toward you "just because." His "just because" relieves you of the burden of striving for His affection and worrying He will fall out of love with you. Today, relax in His grace—His all-embracing love for you—open your arms, and accept His love.

Day 193

Serve Him Best

The LORD will fulfill his purpose for me;
your steadfast love, O LORD, endures forever.
Do not forsake the work of your hands.

PSALM 138:8 NRSV

After years, perhaps decades, of going about life our own way, we conclude that life is meaningless. That's the predictable outcome when we fail to recognize God as our Creator who has given us rules to keep us safe, resources to use for good, and blessings to enjoy and share. Our life's purpose emerges as we let Him lead according to His will and wisdom, because He alone knows where and how we can serve Him best.

Day 194

Gratitude

Give thanks to the Lord, for he is good;
his love endures forever.

PSALM 107:1

Do you regularly count your blessings—the beauty and variety of wildflowers, the immensity of the evening sky, the power of the ocean's waves, the majestic heights of a mountain? Even when you forget to say thank you, God surrounds you with these things every day. Name three things in creation you take pleasure in and give thanks to God for each of them. Your God made them for you simply because He wanted you to enjoy them.

Day 195

Our Life's Diary

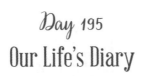

*"Who knows but that you have come to
your royal position for such a time as this?"*

ESTHER 4:14

For those of us who kept a diary when we were young,
we may have filled many pages with passing thoughts
and seemingly insignificant notes. But, looking back, we
realize how God was preparing us to become the women
we are today. The things we experienced, endured, and
encountered fit into God's purpose for our lives. He's
not finished with our life's "diary" yet, but when He is,
we will have reason to rejoice with Him forever.

Day 196

Every Day

Give thanks in all circumstances.

1 Thessalonians 5:18

If you are going through a difficult time in your life, your prayers may sound more like a list of woes than a song of thanksgiving. God wants you to bring to Him your cries of pain, but He also invites you to offer Him your thanks for the good things happening in your life. This is how He reminds you that you and the situation you're facing remain in His hands. Be thankful, because God is present with you—loving and comforting you—every moment of every day.

Day 197
Banishing Loneliness

I am always with you;
you hold me by my right hand.
PSALM 73:23

The ache of loneliness drags us down both physically and emotionally. It saps our energy and burdens our minds with self-doubt and feelings of rejection. God, in His compassion, desires to remove loneliness from our lives by assuring us of His unshakeable, unconquerable love for us. His Spirit, alive in our hearts, reminds us of His presence, offering us the power to banish loneliness and bathe in the tranquility of His devotion and faithfulness to us.

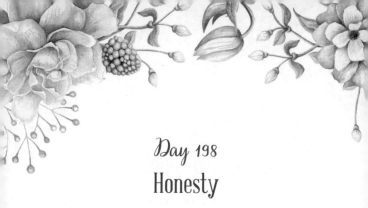

Day 198
Honesty

Good people will be guided by honesty.
PROVERBS 11:3 NCV

Have you ever been tempted to try a little sleight-of-hand—some deception that will give you an edge over someone else or a privilege you want? Even if we pride ourselves on being clever, God calls it something else: dishonest. For all who strive to follow Him, God sets clear directions to guide thought, speech, conduct, and relationships. With the help of the Holy Spirit, commit yourself to honesty in all you say and do.

Day 199
Continuing Relationship

We are many parts of one body,
and we all belong to each other.
ROMANS 12:5 NLT

A sudden life change can throw even the most outgoing person into the throes of loneliness. That's why God may invite us to step forward and reach out to our friends and loved ones who are trying to cope with new circumstances. Our willingness to quietly listen, gently encourage, and kindly guide reflects the way God responds to us whenever we feel lonely. It's His way of nurturing our continuing relationship with Him and with others.

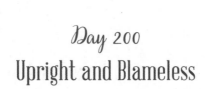

Day 200
Upright and Blameless

Light shines on those who do right;
joy belongs to those who are honest.

PSALM 97:11 NCV

When you're honest and forthright in all things, you never need worry about covering your tracks or being exposed. You can live with a lightness of spirit unknown to those who must glance over their shoulders in fear of being found out. Ask God to show you where you need to act in a more upright and blameless way. With the help of His Spirit working in you, resolve that your relationships and dealings will be marked by godly honesty.

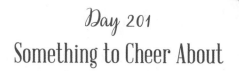

Day 201

Something to Cheer About

You have given up your old way of life with its habits. Each of you is now a new person.

COLOSSIANS 3:9–10 CEV

Hooray for loss when we're talking about destructive behavior, excess weight, or habitual sin! Yet even these losses leave an empty space in our lives, and it's into these spaces that God wishes to enter. Through the power of His Spirit working to change our lives for the better, our loss becomes our gain in self-confidence, satisfaction, and happiness. It's something to cheer about, giving thanks to God, who richly fills our every need.

Day 202

Hope

We who have fled to take hold of the hope set before us may be greatly encouraged. We have this hope as an anchor for the soul, firm and secure.

HEBREWS 6:18–19

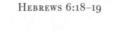

Without hope, you may feel as if you're being swept along by chaotic currents, unable to grasp anything solid. God wants you to know that He is about to reach you, lift you up, and set your feet on the firm ground of His Word and His promises. Though He might not reveal to you the reasons behind current circumstances, He invites you to place your hope in Him, holding firmly and securely to the certainty of His love and care for you.

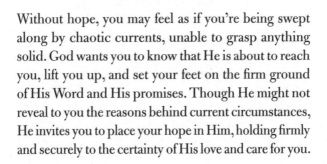

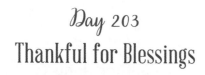

Day 203
Thankful for Blessings

Jesus said to them, "Be careful and guard against all kinds of greed. Life is not measured by how much one owns."

LUKE 12:15 NCV

The recent economic recession has highlighted an important truth. We saw what happens when, instead of worshipping the God who gives us possessions, we worship the possessions. For this sin, as for all others, God sent His Son, Jesus, to win our forgiveness. During His earthly ministry, Jesus showed us how to live as spiritual beings in a material world, contented with what we have, thankful for our blessings, and eager to share with those in need.

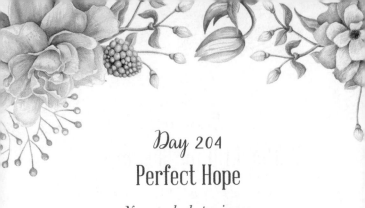

Day 204
Perfect Hope

*No one who hopes in you
will ever be put to shame.*

PSALM 25:3

God has given us His promises in order to provide sure footing in a tumultuous world. He knew we wouldn't be helped by promises filled with ambiguity and double-talk, so He gives it to us straight. *"Put your hope in Me,"* He says, *"and you won't be disappointed."* No one will call you a fool—not after they see your God working on your behalf. Placing your hope in Him is a no-risk proposition, because He will never fail you.

Day 205
Sharing

Honor the LORD with your wealth, with the firstfruits of all your crops; then your barns will be filled to overflowing, and your vats will brim over with new wine.

PROVERBS 3:9–10

Our God-sent material possessions serve to bless our lives with comfort and pleasure. In addition, they provide us with the privilege of blessing the lives of those who have less than we do, sharing with them as God shares with us. We live peacefully and at ease in our world of abundance when we neither covet nor grasp at possessions, but use whatever we have to the glory of God, giving Him thanks and praise.

Day 206

Humility

With humility comes wisdom.

PROVERBS 11:2 NLT

In a misguided desire to appear humble, some people intentionally downplay their abilities and achievements. Your abilities and achievements, however, are unique gifts your God has given to you. Godly humility would have you accept them with pure gratitude and do your best to use them to their fullest. When someone praises you, thank your thoughtful friend then add, "To God be the glory!" This is heavenly humility—and the height of wisdom.

Day 207
He Won't Forget

It is good for me to be near you.
I choose you as my protector.
PSALM 73:28 CEV

Even if it happened years ago, a woman never forgets
the loss of her unborn child—and she doesn't want to.
She knows God asks her to trust His wisdom, but it's
tough to do when the little life growing inside her has
been lost. God knows the tears we shed at each *if only*
that goes through our minds, and He understands the
emptiness we feel, no matter how much time goes by.
He'll never forget—and He doesn't want to.

Day 208

Always Loved

Humility is the fear of the LORD;
its wages are riches and honor and life.

PROVERBS 22:4

Though no one seems eager to pick up a person fallen from the pedestal of pride, God is willing. If you find you have to pick yourself up after a humiliating feat of your own making, know this: God still loves you. He desires to hold you close and help you learn from your experience. Even at your lowest point, you are precious to Him. Give Him your hand and He will help you find your footing again.

Day 209

First Impressions

The heart of the godly thinks
carefully before speaking.
PROVERBS 15:28 NLT

First impressions are powerful, but they're often wrong. The first thing we notice about a person or hear about an event certainly isn't the whole story. Only when we're open to suspending judgment, to welcoming further information, and to allowing more time for observation can we avoid the error of misjudgment. First impressions are intense, impatient to have their way, but the wisest among us will calmly wait until first impressions have given way to facts.

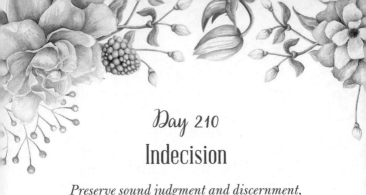

Day 210

Indecision

*Preserve sound judgment and discernment,
do not let them out of your sight; they will be
life for you, an ornament to grace your neck.*

PROVERBS 3:21–22

You don't want to make the wrong decision, so you weigh the pros and cons in your mind over and over, spending sleepless nights wondering what to do. Now would be a good time to stop tossing and turning and put the matter in God's hands. Only He knows the outcome of all possible scenarios. Study His Word on the topic, bring to Him your best thinking on the matter, and open yourself to the guidance of His Spirit. Then make your decision with certainty and confidence.

Day 211
As He Is

*Grow in grace, and in the knowledge
of our Lord and Saviour Jesus Christ.*

2 PETER 3:18 KJV

When we have sinned, we might avoid God because
we think He will punish us. If we believe ourselves
unlovable, we may be drawn to think He couldn't
possibly love us as we are. These misjudgments stand
between us and the God who overflows with kindness
and forgiveness, compassion and gentleness. Try Him,
test Him, and see if these things are true. Doing so will
bring us the peace of knowing our heavenly Father as
He truly is.

Day 212
Goodness Revealed

I will praise the LORD, who counsels me;
even at night my heart instructs me.

PSALM 16:7

When you're faced with a decision, you have a wise counselor in God's Word. Open the Bible, because in it God has revealed His will and His guidelines for the lives of His people, a necessary foundation for any good decision. You also have a wise counselor in His Holy Spirit. Let Him teach you how to pray about the decision you need to make. When you do these things, you will discover His answer.

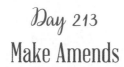

Day 213
Make Amends

*As far as the east is from the west, so far has [God]
removed our transgressions from us.*
PSALM 103:12 NKJV

How we hate to make mistakes! But now is the time to
step back, own up to our actions, and make amends
where possible. Then we can step forward, leaving
the mistake far behind. Because Jesus has brought us
into relationship with our heavenly Father, that's the
way God treats our sins: After we've confessed and
received His pardon, He puts the sin behind us, urging
us to continue our journey as cleansed, forgiven, and
beloved women of God.

Day 214

Intolerance

*What does the LORD require of you? To act justly and
to love mercy and to walk humbly with your God.*

MICAH 6:8

When you find yourself easily irritated by others, God
wants you to look within yourself. Take stock of your
feelings and make an honest assessment of your attitude.
With the help of the Holy Spirit, turn away from intolerance. Let His Spirit work in you a heart of compassion,
a heart willing to forgive, to accept differences, and to
walk humbly with your God.

Day 215

Everything Will Be Okay

*Everyone has sinned and is far away from God's
saving presence. But by the free gift of God's grace
all are put right with him through Christ Jesus.*

ROMANS 3:23–24 GNT

All of us make mistakes, but God never does. In fact, He
has the power to turn our mistakes around, so even those
things we have badly botched end up working for our
good. Humble admission of our guilt and unconditional
faith in His forgiveness through Jesus Christ gets God
working on our behalf, and when He's in charge, we
can take a deep breath and relax, knowing everything
will turn out okay in the end.

Day 216

Intolerance

It is a sin to despise ones neighbor,
but blessed is the one who is kind to the needy.

PROVERBS 14:21

Even in the most conscientious heart, intolerance finds a place to fester. It can raise its ugly head with one disapproving thought of "those people." Invite the Holy Spirit into your heart to banish any feelings of intolerance you may harbor. Ask Him to open your spiritual eyes so you will see God's presence in others, finding Him reflected in their eyes as He is reflected in yours. Then think of "those people" accordingly— as children of God created in His image.

Day 217
Financial Resources

"You cannot serve both God and money."
Luke 16:13 gnt

Few issues cause more anxiety than those concerning money. The stress begins when we forget that money is a resource provided by God, not a substitute for Him. He willingly gives us what He knows is best for us and, guided by His Spirit, we manage our financial resources wisely and well. There's nothing to worry about, because our security rests with the giver, not the gift. Our spirit finds peace in Him alone.

Day 218

Laughter

"[God] will yet fill your mouth with
laughter and your lips with shouts of joy."

JOB 8:21

The old saying might ring true for you right now:
"Laugh and the world laughs with you; cry and you
cry alone." Yet you know you're not alone when you
weep. God remains at your side with the comfort of
His peace, relief, and yes, laughter. Seem impossible?
Not with God. Not when you immerse yourself in His
presence today and bathe in the certainty of a better
tomorrow. Let Him fill your life with laughter!

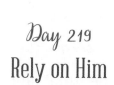

Day 219
Rely on Him

"Lay up for yourselves treasures in heaven."
MATTHEW 6:20 NKJV

During His earthly ministry, Jesus shared with all who would listen, then and now, about greed, discontent, and indebtedness—the unsettling consequences of a wrong relationship with money. He urges us to rely on Him to provide, because He knows how much money we need and why we need it. When our relationship with Him stands on unwavering trust in His faithfulness, our relationship with money rests easy in our hearts and minds.

Day 220

Genuine Joy

My. . .sisters, be full of joy in the Lord.
PHILIPPIANS 3:1 NCV

If you have placed your hope and faith in God, you have every reason to be happy. You know who you are and whose you are. You have set your heart on doing His will, and you hold to His promises to protect and preserve you in any situation you may face in life. Take a moment to thank Him for bringing you into the light of His love, and cultivate a spirit of genuine joy.

Day 221

God's Commandments

Don't be immoral in matters of sex.
That is a sin against your own body
in a way that no other sin is.

1 Corinthians 6:18 CEV

At a certain age, we might avoid looking in a mirror under a strong light! Even more uncomfortable, however, is examining our lifestyle under the glare of God's commandments. Where the blemish of immorality or the wrinkle of sin exists, God yearns to renew us with His full pardon, earned for us by His Son, Jesus. Through the power of His Spirit, He restores us to Himself as flawless and holy, completely beautiful in His sight.

Day 222
Leadership

The greatest among you should be like the youngest,
and the one who rules like the one who serves.

LUKE 22:26

No matter what your role in life, you're a leader. Either your words and actions lead people toward goodness and virtue, or your conduct turns people away. For this reason, God gives this advice, "Lead by being as happy to walk with the weakest as with the strongest. Lead by being as happy to serve others in an unnoticed, unsung capacity as to take center stage." Follow the example of Christ who comforted even His enemies.

Day 223

The Reason

*Your hands have made me and fashioned
me; give me understanding, that I may
learn Your commandments.*

PSALM 119:73 NKJV

God treats us as His beloved daughters, and He has no
wish to keep us away from what will make us truly happy.
When our desires clash with His commandments, we
find our peace in knowing He's keeping us safe in body
and spirit. We rest in the arms of one who can see the
sad end of the world's careless ways. When God says
no, He says it for a reason, and the reason is love.

Day 224
Blessing Others

Follow my example, as I
follow the example of Christ.

1 CORINTHIANS 11:1

If you want to learn about leadership, look at the life of Jesus Christ. Though the Son of God, He did not use His status to intimidate others or amass power, but to serve both the powerful and the weak. This is the example Jesus has set for you. Never shirk your responsibility to those beneath you in authority, education, or social status. Instead, do everything you can to bless the lives of others.

Day 225

The Fullness of His Spirit

You want me to be completely
truthful, so teach me wisdom.

PSALM 51:6 NCV

When something we did appears all right but leaves us feeling uneasy, God may be prompting us to question our motivation. Even better than we can ourselves, God can read our hearts. If He finds self-interest, lust, or hostility hidden there, He desires to draw it out so we can enjoy the fullness of His Spirit dwelling within us. With the assurance of His pardon, we can confidently confide even our deepest motivations in His presence.

Day 226
Loneliness

A father to the fatherless, a defender
of widows, is God in his holy dwelling.
God sets the lonely in families.

Psalm 68:5–6

No one has come to take the place of the one no longer in your life, and you're not sure anyone really could. You ache with loneliness. These days are tough, and they're not days God wants to prolong. He sends people—relatives, friends, even strangers sometimes—to lift loneliness from you and bring you into the company and companionship of others. Ask Him to open your eyes and heart to those He sends to comfort you.

Day 227
The Drive

Whatever you do, work at it with all your heart, as though you were working for the Lord and not for people.

COLOSSIANS 3:23 GNT

What motivates us matters. That's why God calls us to complete obedience to Him and loving service to others as our motivation in all things. It's why we get up in the morning, and it's the drive behind our thoughts, actions, and decisions. It's how we can go to bed at night in peace, because no matter where the day took us, we did everything to the best of our ability and to the glory of God and our neighbor.

Day 228

Never Alone

[God said,] "Never will I leave you;
never will I forsake you."

HEBREWS 13:5

You know what it's like to feel lonely in a crowd, because you feel that way right now. Even though many people surround you, you realize not one of them truly understands what you're going through. But do you believe God understands you—truly understands? He does, you know. And He yearns for you to let Him fill your loneliness with His presence and the fullness of His compassion and care.

Day 229
God's Rules

This is the love of God, that we keep his commandments: and his commandments are not grievous.

1 JOHN 5:3 KJV

On the books of countless communities and organizations are outdated, irrelevant rules. The same *cannot* be said of the rules governing morality that God has set down in His book, the Bible. Because the human heart has not changed with time, God's rules apply to us as surely as they did to His people of ages past. Then as now, willing and joyful obedience in the things we think, say, and do every day brings us closer to God.

Day 230

Loss

I consider everything a loss
because of the surpassing worth
of knowing Christ Jesus my Lord.

PHILIPPIANS 3:8

You've lost something or someone that meant the world to you, and now all you can see is a big hole where your future used to be. If you let God step into that big hole, you'll see Him fill it up, spill out, and tower over it. Where emptiness scared you moments before, abundance invites you now. God asks you to come with Him while He walks you safely through your sorrow and makes of it a renewed tomorrow and a new future.

Day 231

The Fence of Freedom

If you look carefully into the perfect law that
sets you free, and if you do what it says. . .
then God will bless you for doing it.

JAMES 1:25 NLT

Like a fence that protects a beautiful garden, God sets
around us the barrier of His standards. This allows
us to enjoy our lives and our relationships within the
bounds of God's good intentions for us, and it protects
us from destructive habits, attitudes, and behaviors.
We can look at God's standards as a fence of freedom.
Because it keeps us away from sin, we are free to grow
abundantly in peace, love, and happiness.

Day 232
Unimagined Plans

"Whoever finds their life will lose it, and whoever loses their life for my sake will find it."

MATTHEW 10:39

Perhaps you have never told anyone how many of your dreams and desires you have given up for the sake of doing God's will. When it comes to sacrifice, few answer His call, but you did. He knows, and because you have suffered the calculated loss of your own plans and agenda, you will find your gains to be more than you could have imagined possible.

Day 233

Dissolve the Darkness

"The world will make you suffer.
But be brave! I have defeated the world!"

John 16:33 GNT

Like a shadow, a troubled past can darken the present with disturbing thoughts and distressing memories. God, who was there with us, knows what happened; and even more, He knows why He permitted it to happen. We can pour out our pain to Him, hiding none of our feelings. Then allow Him to dissolve the darkness with the light of His healing touch and lift the gloom of painful memories. "Why?" is His; but peace is ours.

Day 234

Ministry

*He has made us competent as ministers of a new
covenant—not of the letter but of the Spirit;
for the letter kills, but the Spirit gives life.*

2 Corinthians 3:6

Caring for and comforting others is a profound privilege.
With God's Spirit at work in you, let your everyday
words and actions comfort and bless others just as God
has comforted and blessed you. Your ministry makes
you a love-sharer rather than a lawgiver. Maybe you feel
you have nothing to share with others, but you do. God
loves you, and knowing that enables you to love others.

Day 235

A New Course

Understanding your word brings
light to the minds of ordinary people.

PSALM 119:130 CEV

We wish things had been different, but they weren't. Now what? Though we cannot remake the past, God has given us today to decide on a new course, to lay a fresh foundation. This time, we know to take Him into our confidence as we think about our future and plan how to get there. This time, even if we need to work a little harder, we will make it, because our strong advocate is also our support and guide.

Day 236
Comfort and Confidence

*"When you give a banquet, invite the poor,
the crippled, the lame, the blind, and you will be
blessed. Although they cannot repay you, you will
be repaid at the resurrection of the righteous."*

LUKE 14:13-14

Complaints and criticisms hurt, and you might just as soon serve only those people who know how to say thank you. Rest assured God hears you. He knows what it's like to shower people with blessings only to have them congratulate themselves for their good fortune. Yet He continues to bless, and He invites you to follow Him in His ministry. You will hear His comforting thank-you, because He knows.

Day 237

The Perfect Answer

You will keep in perfect peace all who trust in you, all whose thoughts are fixed on you!

ISAIAH 26:3 NLT

Most of us have an impression of an ideal woman that glows in our mind's eye. But in most cases, we're frustrated for we have yet to reach her level of perfection. Our God reaches out to us with a smile, because He yearns to relieve us of the burden of perfectionism. He adores the women we really are—windblown hair, smudged mascara, chipped fingernails, and all! Let's allow Him to free us to love the women we really are, and in doing so, wrap ourselves up in His wonderful peace. God is the perfect answer to perfectionism.

Day 238

Mistakes

Happy is the person whose sins are forgiven,
whose wrongs are pardoned.

Psalm 32:1 ncv

Admitting guilt isn't easy for anyone. It's uncomfortable and embarrassing, but when we take full responsibility for our sins God can bring us comfort and confidence. You too have made mistakes; we all have. The good news is that we aren't doomed by the mistakes we've made—not at all. With God there is room for pardon. Tell Him about your mistakes, and let Him help you find a new beginning.

Day 239

His Perfection

By one sacrifice [Jesus Christ] has made
perfect forever those who are being made holy.
HEBREWS 10:14

The only perfect, sinless person to walk among us was
Jesus Christ. Through His acts of healing, kindness,
and mercy, He set an example for us to follow. Our
Lord begs us not to burden ourselves by grasping at our
concept of perfection, or suffering because of the flaws
we see around us. Christ's genuine perfection is ours
to receive. It is His perfection that we possess through
faith in His life, death, and resurrection.

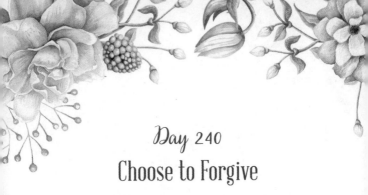

Day 240
Choose to Forgive

[Jesus said,] "Forgive us our sins, as we have forgiven those who sin against us."

<small>MATTHEW 6:12 NLT</small>

The weaknesses, mistakes, and sins of others affect your life, sometimes bringing serious and lasting harm to you and those you love. You have a right to feel angry, but God offers a better alternative. He urges you to forgive, because forgiveness is the only way to prevent bitterness from taking root in your soul. Compare the "right" of bitterness and the privilege of forgiveness. Choose to forgive.

Day 241

Together

"I will never leave you nor forsake you."

JOSHUA 1:5

At one time or another, most of us have prayed for God to get us out of a tough situation. But He didn't. Why? Because it's possible His hand was outstretched for ours so that the two of us could walk through it together. With Him, we have an infinite source of support, power, strength, and wisdom in any and all situations. As His daughters, we possess the promise of His presence wherever the path may lead, and the assurance of triumph, because our victory rests in Him.

Day 242
Money

*My God will meet all your needs according
to the riches of his glory in Christ Jesus.*

<small>PHILIPPIANS 4:19</small>

God knows how you feel when money runs out at the
end of the month. He has compassion on you in your
concern for those dependent on your ability to meet
their needs. Let Him remind you of something: He's in
the need-meeting business too. The God who long ago
met your most pressing spiritual need does not abandon
you in this, your earthly need. Take all your needs to
Him in prayer, for He hears and answers.

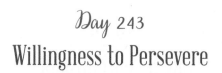

Day 243

Willingness to Persevere

Let endurance have its full effect,
so that you may be mature and
complete, lacking in nothing.

JAMES 1:4 NRSV

The way of faith isn't always calm. Disquieting times of spiritual apathy, dryness, doubt, and even persecution make us wonder if it's all worth it. God may send these kinds of tests our way, because we need to discover the strength of our commitment to Him. Our willingness to persevere in prayer, meditation, and Bible study affirms us as we find more and more peace, joy, and confidence as women of God.

Day 244

Rich Contentment

*Keep your lives free from the love of money
and be content with what you have.*

HEBREWS 13:5

God doesn't ask you to live without money, but He warns you against the love of money. He wants to free you from the spiritually corrosive sins of greed and envy, and He wants to release you from the bondage of a never-ending list of must-haves. Turn from a love of money and the things it can buy. Ask His Spirit in you to become your most cherished possession, and you will find a rich contentment in everything.

Day 245

The Whisper of His Spirit

Continue in prayer, and watch
in the same with thanksgiving.

COLOSSIANS 4:2 KJV

It isn't difficult to understand why at times we feel awkward praying. After all, how do we know we're not chattering into thin air? But even in our doubt, God encourages us to pour out our deepest thoughts to Him and then to listen. We stop speaking and wait for the whisper of His Spirit to enter our consciousness. Then we hear Him assure us of His presence and gently invite us to continue our conversation with Him.

Day 246
Motives

Serve him with wholehearted devotion and with a willing mind, for the LORD searches every heart and understands every desire and every thought.

1 CHRONICLES 28:9

We claim publicly we're asking for no reward but seek acclaim privately when no reward comes our way. If you find yourself harboring offense, check the motives behind your charitable acts. God already has. Ask Him to replace selfish motives with selfless ones and to instill in you a spirit of compassion, kindness, and generosity. On the outside, you'll continue doing the good things you've been doing. On the inside, you'll be doing them for the right reason.

Day 247

The Sweet Sound

What other nation is so great as to have their
*gods near them the way the L*ORD *our God*
is near us whenever we pray to him?

DEUTERONOMY 4:7

When we pray, do we kneel or stand? Do we speak
in words that have echoed through the ages, or in the
spontaneous utterances of our own hearts? Do we hold
our thoughts for a private time with Him, or speak to Him
in the workplace or as we go about our daily activities? Let
none of these things disturb us however, whenever, or
wherever we pray. Because God is interested in only
one thing: the sweet sound of our voices.

Day 248

Best Interest

Pursue righteousness, faith,
love and peace, along with those who
call on the Lord out of a pure heart.

2 TIMOTHY 2:22

Though your motives are pure toward others, you will encounter those whose hearts aren't pure, and it hurts to find out someone has used you for their own purposes. When that happens—and it almost certainly will at one time or another—take comfort in God. You can be sure that even when others are untrue, God never wavers. He is always thinking of you, putting your best interest first.

Who We Really Are

Be honest in your evaluation of
yourselves, measuring yourselves
by the faith God has given us.

ROMANS 12:3 NLT

While our pride suggests that the problem rests with others, God's Spirit tells the truth. He does this not to condemn us, but to draw us to the knowledge of who we really are. In Him, we have no need to set ourselves above others or envy their praise and applause. While He reaches down to us with His peace, we receive the joy of reaching across to others as beloved sisters and brothers in the family of God.

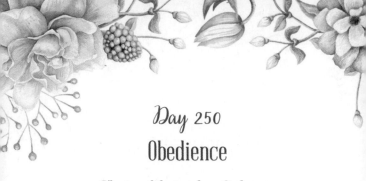

Day 250

Obedience

*The proof that we love God comes
when we keep his commandments
and they are not at all troublesome.*

1 JOHN 5:3 MSG

If you have broken one of God's commandments and now see the reason why He put that commandment there in the first place, you've learned an important lesson. Why repeat it? He has given you His commandments not to burden you with outdated rules and undue regulations but for your physical, emotional, and spiritual well-being. Embrace all His commandments and obey them, and you will live in the full freedom He intends for you.

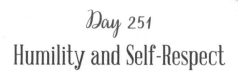

Day 251

Humility and Self-Respect

When pride comes, then comes disgrace,
but with humility comes wisdom.

PROVERBS 11:2

Healthy pride gives us the ability to stand tall, but unhealthy pride makes us think we tower over others. All our relationships suffer, including our relationship with God. That's why He urges us to let Him root out self-importance wherever it lurks, replacing it with genuine humility and godly self-respect. Then we can take our rightful place with and among others, our relationships marked by generosity, peace, mutual support, encouragement, and delight.

Day 252

Sincere and Humble

If anyone obeys his word, love for
God is truly made complete in them.
This is how we know we are in him.

1 JOHN 2:5

If a camera were to record your every word and action today, what would those watching the film learn about you? Would they be able to see that you love God, that you belong to Him? God is pure and holy and when we strive to live by the commandments He's given us with sincere and humble hearts, others see the resemblance. They can tell that we are His children.

Day 253

Inner Peace

We remember before our God and Father your work produced by faith, your labor prompted by love, and your endurance inspired by hope in our Lord Jesus Christ.

1 THESSALONIANS 1:3

Sometimes sticking to biblical principles brings not peace but friction. Yet the friction exists only on the outside, because inside, we're standing on the firm foundation of God's commandments. Our inner peace depends not on the applause of friends and loved ones who have chosen another way, but on the approval of God, who has our safety, security, and spiritual prosperity at heart. He is the source of lasting peace!

Day 254

Obstacles

God will strengthen you with his own great
power so that you will not give up when
troubles come, but you will be patient.

COLOSSIANS 1:11 NCV

Perhaps you are facing a mountain in your life—a circumstance so tall and fierce that you have given up before you even started. You're sure there is no way around it, no solution, no hope for you. Take comfort in the fact that you are not facing your mountain alone. God is with you. While your strength is small, God's is great. He may lead you around, over, or help you carve a path right through the middle. Take His hand and somehow you will overcome.

Day 255
His Principles

The fruit of the Spirit is love, joy, peace, forbearance,
kindness, goodness, faithfulness, gentleness and
self-control. Against such things there is no law.

If we desire peace, the God of peace draws us to live
by His principles. His commandments are designed
to guide us along His path so that we can avoid the
pitfalls of sin. His Spirit works within us to keep our
hearts and minds in Him and away from the conflicts
of envy, greed, and arrogance. God's Son, Jesus, holds
out to us a right relationship with Him, one marked
by faith, trust, and love. By following His principles,
peace is yours.

Day 256
Never Sleeps

He will not let you be defeated.
He who guards you never sleeps.
PSALM 121:3 NCV

Discrimination. Ridicule. Mockery. The obstacles towering in front of you look insurmountable. From your vantage point, if you were to stray just a little from God's way, you could get around the problem and minimize its effect on your life. But consider God's vantage point. He has traveled this way before you, and He knows there are no safe detours. Trust Him to lead you to the other side the right way—His way.

Day 257

What Comes First

*"Seek first God's kingdom and what God wants.
Then all your other needs will be met as well."*

Matthew 6:33 ncv

If all we need to do each day leaves us drained and discouraged, it's time to talk with God about our priorities. He invites us to put Him first in mind, heart, and action; and then He promises us that everything else will fall into place. When His priorities guide our decisions, it's easy to separate real responsibilities from those things that steal our time and energy. No more frustration! Only the peace and pleasure of knowing what comes first.

Day 258
Offenses

"I have swept away your offenses like a cloud,
your sins like the morning mist."

ISAIAH 44:22

If you have ever watched the morning sun burn away the fog, recall the image when you come before God in prayer. Any offense against God you have ever committed—either intentionally or unintentionally—has been burned away in the light of His forgiveness. Offenses no longer cover you, and guilt no longer shrouds your heart. God has done this for you because He loves you. Respond in joyous thanksgiving today!

Day 259
What Really Matters

"Choose this day whom you will serve. . .but as
for me and my household, we will serve the LORD."

JOSHUA 24:15 NRSV

If God sets our priorities, we know what's truly important. We're able to resist the pull of selfish impulses and empty distractions. We receive His Spirit to guide us toward lasting goals, such as love for God and others, and we have His perspective on where our time and attention is best directed. At the end of the day, we lie down fulfilled and satisfied because we've thought, said, and done those things that really matter.

Day 260
Real Love

Love makes up for all offenses.
PROVERBS 10:12 NLT

False love denies offenses and lives an illusion, but real love acknowledges the offense—and covers it with a compassionate, forgiving heart. Blind love says "nothing happened" and hides in the shadows, but real love says "I forgive you" and begins a new day. What kind of love do you show toward others? Pray for real love, the kind of love God has first shown you. Real love covers. Real love forgives. Real love lasts for eternity.

Day 261

A New Response

*Don't become angry quickly,
because getting angry is foolish.*

ECCLESIASTES 7:9 NCV

Someone knows all the right buttons to push! While we're tempted to react in kind, we know our anger will only escalate the argument. God's way offers us a new response, a response that might never change our tormentor, but will certainly change us. His way strengthens us to meet provocation with His Spirit of patience and kindness, forgiveness and love. With Him, our peace is assured. And who knows? It might rub off on you-know-who!

Day 262
Past

*This is what GOD says. . . "Forget about what's
happened; don't keep going over old history."*
ISAIAH 43:16, 18 MSG

A parent, a child, a spouse just can't forget—and won't
let you forget either. Or maybe it's the other way around.
In either case, the past is poisoning the present. Invite
God into the picture and ask Him to help you apply
His antidote to this cycle of unhealthy and hurtful
arguments and accusations. His antidote? Repentance.
Forgiveness. Commitment to put the past behind you.
God's comfort thrives even in the midst of conflict.

Power to Bring Peace

[Love] keeps no record of being wronged.

1 Corinthians 13:5 nlt

God is love, but He hates sin. Sin, incompatible with His holiness, provokes Him to rightful anger, but then His love steps in. Out of love, His Son, Jesus, faced God's anger for us by winning our complete forgiveness through His life, death, and resurrection. With His Spirit alive in our hearts, we too meet provocation with patience. We too hate provocative behavior but love the person. We too have the power to bring peace.

Day 264
A New Eternity

*Forgetting the past and straining toward
what is ahead, I keep trying to reach the
goal and get the prize for which God called
me through Christ to the life above.*

PHILIPPIANS 3:13–14 NCV

Your past continues to haunt you. Why wouldn't it? What
you did and who you were back then leave nothing but
shameful memories. God was there too and He saw
everything. He is here now, however, and He sees an
older, wiser, and completely forgiven child of God. His
forgiveness gives you the go-ahead to continue with
your life, renewed and energized, with your focus on
Him and a new eternity.

Day 265

Caring Counselor

Let the wicked. . .turn to the LORD that
he may have mercy on them. Yes, turn to
our God, for he will forgive generously.

ISAIAH 55:7 NLT

In the course of growing up, many of us went through a stage of rebellion. Often under the guidance of a parent or teacher, however, we matured, and our troubled spirits found peace. Whenever we take a stand against God, He reveals Himself to us as our compassionate Father and caring Counselor. He has no interest in punishing us, but in entering our hearts and minds so we can continue growing in spiritual maturity, holiness, and grace.

Day 266

Patience

Patience is better than strength.

PROVERBS 16:32 NCV

"I'm not a patient person!" You've heard it said, and
perhaps you've even said it yourself. Unfortunately, the
statement supports a false idea about patience. Rather
than an inborn personality trait given only to some,
patience is a gift of the Holy Spirit worked in the hearts
of those who love Him. Godly patience allows you to
respond to life's trying situations with serenity and
self-control, sure evidence of your continuing walk
with God.

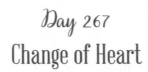

Day 267

Change of Heart

I will cleanse them from all the guilt of their sin
against me, and I will forgive all the guilt of
their sin and rebellion against me.

JEREMIAH 33:8 NRSV

When a loved one rebels against our godly principles and values, we hurt. We hurt for the person who stubbornly clings to a destructive lifestyle, and we hurt for ourselves because we had higher hopes and expectations. Our prayers to God go to one who shares our hurt and understands what rebellion against good feels like. As we pray, we can find our comfort in believing that forgiveness is available and a change of heart possible for every erring soul.

Day 268
Godly Patience

Let us not become weary in doing good,
for at the proper time we will reap
a harvest if we do not give up.

GALATIANS 6:9

Things aren't happening quickly enough, and you're feeling frustrated. Pause for a moment and compare your timetable with God's timetable. Evidently they don't match! Instead of fighting against His gracious will, put your trust in it. Let Him unfold the hours, days, and years to you in His own time. His time is, without fail, the right time. Learn from Him the difference godly patience can work in your heart, mind, and spirit.

Day 269

Genuine Peace

"The LORD has made a solemn promise,
and he will not abandon you, for he has
decided to make you his own people."

1 SAMUEL 12:22 GNT

We make many decisions, some of which we later regret. While healthy regret probes our thinking and motivation so we don't make the same mistake again, unhealthy regret stirs up anguish of heart and mind, often still potent years after the event. Our prayers to God for help with regret permits Him to lift its onerous burden and draw us to genuine acceptance. Acceptance stands as His bridge between unhealthy regret and genuine peace.

Day 270
Peace

You, LORD, give true peace to those who depend on you, because they trust you.

ISAIAH 26:3 NCV

Daily stress, nagging worries, and ceaseless squabbles make you long for a place—an hour—of peace. You don't need to look for a serene spot, however, and you don't need to arrange a special time to rest your heart in God's peace. He has it for you right now, right where you are. Give God all those things that drive out peace—name them, hand them over, and don't grab them back again! Then take comfort in the peace He has for you.

Day 271

Renew and Restore

Godly sorrow brings repentance that
leads to salvation and leaves no regret.

2 CORINTHIANS 7:10

Now that we're faced with the consequences, we wish we could go back and undo everything! But God restricts us to this time and this place. Genuine regret over past mistakes has the power to bring us to God today, and it's here and now that He extends His hands in forgiveness. As He pardons us, He offers to guide us through our unhappy circumstances, for He has the desire to renew and restore His peace to the humble, repentant heart.

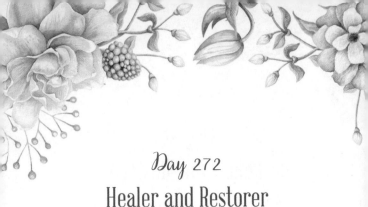

Day 272

Healer and Restorer

A heart at peace gives life to the body.

PROVERBS 14:30

Without question, mind and body are linked. God made us that way! His gift of spiritual peace not only soothes a troubled mind by replacing worry with trust, fear with faith, but it also permits a tired, nervous body to get a good night's sleep. Let God fight the battles taking place in your mind, and let your heart rest in His peace. Commit yourself to Him, the healer and restorer of life.

Day 273

Centered in God's Love

Peacemakers who sow in peace
reap a harvest of righteousness.
JAMES 3:18

When an argument flares between us and a friend or loved one, our stress level skyrockets. We can take steps to restore harmony by asking God to help us pinpoint the real problem. His perspective lets us differentiate simple misunderstandings from complex issues, and His guidance works toward healing for us and the others involved. Relationships are worth the work it takes to keep them strong—and our prayers to keep them centered in God's love.

Day 274

Perfection

All have sinned and fall short of the glory of God,
and all are justified freely by his grace through
the redemption that came by Christ Jesus.

ROMANS 3:23-24

You may have spent years trying to reach perfection, but perfection remains out of your grasp. Your futile striving has landed you right where God wants you—in His arms, admitting your utter lack of power to make yourself perfect. Now you're ready to hear what He has done for you. Long ago, He declared you perfect by sending Jesus Christ to remove your imperfections. Only He has the power to do so, and He did.

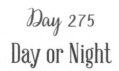

Day 275

Day or Night

[Jesus said,] "I stand at the door and knock.
If you hear my voice and open the door,
I will come in and eat with you."

REVELATION 3:20 NCV

No earthy relationship thrives without effort on our part to keep it healthy, lively, and strong. Our relationship with Jesus Christ is no different. While He has initiated the relationship, our Spirit-prompted response transforms it into a meaningful and significant part of our lives. Christ's presence, like that of a faithful friend, is something we can rely on. He is someone we can call on, day or night. It's the relationship of a lifetime—and beyond.

Day 276

Boundless Perfection

To all perfection I see a limit;
but your commands are boundless.

PSALM 119:96

You may look with awe at the perfection of the stars on a dark, clear night, and melt in joy at the sight of a newborn's perfect eyes, ears, fingers, and toes. With the same sense of wonder, consider God's commandments, spoken by God for your daily guidance and eternal good. He sets His commandments before you this day, inviting you to meditate on the boundless perfection of His words and take them, in their entirety, into your heart.

Day 277
Building Blocks

People. . .might say that you are doing wrong.
Live such good lives that they will see the good
things you do and will give glory to God.

1 PETER 2:12 NCV

Perhaps the good name we carry has suffered because of some past behavior or malicious tale passed around by others. Whatever the case, God's principles are the building blocks that can help us regain what has been lost. Our day-to-day obedience to Him reveals the lie behind false rumors and shows everyone who knows us the kind of person we really are. We won't need to worry about what we did or what others say; our God-guided actions will tell our new and true story.

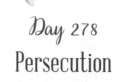

Day 278

Persecution

Who shall separate us from the love of Christ?
Shall trouble or hardship or persecution or
famine or nakedness or danger or sword? . . .
No, in all these things we are more than
conquerors through him who loved us.

ROMANS 8:35, 37

As the Holy Spirit immerses your soul in the sweetness of God's love, your attitude and behavior undergo noticeable changes. Now you're more discerning in your choices and more thoughtful about what you say and do. Some people, however, will clamor for the "old you" back, even resorting to name-calling and slander when you refuse. Don't let their persecution sway you, but call on God, whose strength and comfort are yours in all situations you face.

Day 279
Women of God

We are careful to be honorable before the Lord,
but we also want everyone else to
see that we are honorable.

2 Corinthians 8:21 NLT

The reputation we carry as women of good character is worth keeping. It contributes to our emotional well-being, our ability to make friends with other people of godly character, and our eligibility for responsible positions in church, business, and the community. Even more important, however, is the reputation we carry as women of God. It's a reputation gained among others when they see our spiritual commitment carried out in words and actions of kindness, compassion, and love.

Day 280
Public Applause

Everyone who wants to live a godly
life in Christ Jesus will be persecuted.

2 TIMOTHY 3:12

You know how it is when someone is successful; many times people will applaud them publicly while saying and doing hurtful things behind their backs. When you begin to live a life of peace and joy as God's child, there will be those who will smile to your face but secretly resent you for it. When that happens, you must forgive. Use those situations as opportunities to let others know that they can have what you have. All they have to do is ask.

Day 281
Downtime

*Thus said the Lord G*OD*, the Holy One of Israel:*
In returning and rest you shall be saved;
in quietness and in trust shall be your strength.

ISAIAH 30:15 NRSV

Sometimes we're so busy meeting the demands of others that we have little or no downtime. While it's good and God-pleasing to carry out our responsibilities each day, there's a danger when outside demands threaten our inner peace. Jesus, in His earthly ministry, took time out from His teaching and preaching to pray to His heavenly Father. In doing so, He set an example that applies today, especially when we feel burdened with way too much to do.

Day 282
Perspective

"My thoughts are not your thoughts, neither are your ways my ways," declares the Lord. "As the heavens are higher than the earth, so are my ways higher than your ways and my thoughts than your thoughts."

ISAIAH 55:8–9

"We plan, God laughs." While the saying gets a chuckle, we're usually not chuckling when our plans go awry. But step back and look at the situation from another perspective—God's perspective. He sees your future as clearly as He sees your past and present, and He knows how to get you from here to there. Ask the Holy Spirit to help you look from God's perspective—and laugh with the joy of knowing you remain under His watchful care!

Day 283
Votes of Confidence

*We must try to become mature and start
thinking about more than just the basic
things we were taught about Christ.*

HEBREWS 6:1 CEV

Because she has confidence in her, a mother gives her daughter greater responsibilities. Similarly, God grants us increasing responsibilities as we mature spiritually and learn how to put His will into practice. From our responsibility to God to thank and praise Him, to our responsibility to others to love and care for them, God's Spirit gives us the privilege of taking on more and more. We should rejoice in the many votes of confidence our God has given us!

Day 284
Selfish Desires

Do not be shaped by this world; instead be
changed within by a new way of thinking.
Then you will be able to decide what God
wants for you; you will know what is good
and pleasing to him and what is perfect.

ROMANS 12:2 NCV

When you live for the moment, your perspective
focuses on what will bring you instant pleasure and
immediate gratification. The Holy Spirit has opened
to you a deeper, longer, and broader perspective—an
eternal perspective. Now you're disposed to put aside
selfish desires in favor of godly choices, and you're
willing to weigh the spiritual consequences of your
actions. Practice seeing with an eternal perspective
every day, and prepare to notice eternal results.

Day 285

In Faith and Confidence

If any of you is lacking in wisdom,
ask God, who gives to all generously and
ungrudgingly, and it will be given you.

JAMES 1:5 NRSV

Action involves risk, and many of us are uncomfortable with risk. But if we never take action, we certainly will lose opportunities, bypass relationships, and block the way to a joyful, satisfying life. God helps us handle risk by giving us the power to reason, weigh pros and cons, and consult with others as well as God, and then to step forward in faith and confidence when we have reached our best decision. And whatever the outcome, He will be there with us.

Day 286
Pleasing God

Our only goal is to please God.

2 CORINTHIANS 5:9 NCV

When you have a specific goal in mind, you take every opportunity and use every resource available to you to reach your goal. The goal of living a God-pleasing life is no different. Look for opportunities in your day to do those things you know God wants you to do. Use the resources you have on hand right now to strengthen your faith, increase your understanding of His Word, and serve others with Christlike love in your heart.

Day 287
Certainty

Unto thee, O LORD, do I lift up my soul.
O my God, I trust in thee: let me not be ashamed.

PSALM 25:1–2 KJV

There are risks involved in loving God. We risk having to say no to desires that are contrary to God's will for us. We risk the ridicule of those who prefer their own perspective to God's wisdom, and we risk times of trial and testing. But here's where certainty steps in: By trusting in and loving Him, we gain a purposeful and meaningful life as a spiritually mature woman of God, able to receive His blessings with pure gladness and experience His peace with unfettered joy.

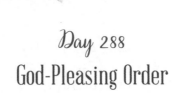

Day 288

God-Pleasing Order

Beloved, if our heart condemn us not, then have we confidence toward God. And whatsoever we ask, we receive of him, because we keep his commandments, and do those things that are pleasing in his sight.

1 JOHN 3:21–22 KJV

If you have been waiting to get your life in order before you focus on pleasing God, God has a happy surprise for you. God has put your life in order through the earthly ministry of Jesus. As His forgiven child, respond in genuine joy and gratitude by living to please Him. Worship Him, obey His commandments, and show compassion on others. By focusing on pleasing God, you will find your life in God-pleasing order.

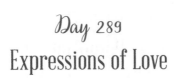

Day 289

Expressions of Love

"I tell you the truth, anything you did for even the least of my people here, you also did for me."

MATTHEW 25:40 NCV

A sacrifice is a choice made for a higher good. We sacrifice our resources to share with our loved ones, and we sacrifice our time to help someone in need. While we might grumble occasionally at the sacrifices we make, God's Spirit moves us to see them as expressions of love, for that's what they are. More than a lifetime of grasping to get what we want, sacrificing to serve others brings meaning to life and heart-deep fulfillment and joy.

Day 290
Potential

I have filled him with the Spirit of God,
with wisdom, with understanding,
with knowledge and with all kinds of skills.

EXODUS 31:3

Have you reached your full potential? If you're still breathing, you haven't! God has blessed you with a wide range of talents for you to tap throughout your life. Enrich every stage of your life by following your interests, broadening your knowledge, and developing your abilities. You will be surprised at the variety of God-given gifts you possess—and experience the sheer enjoyment of embracing your potential.

Day 291
Nurturing

Christ is the sacrifice that takes away our
sins and the sins of all the world's people.

1 JOHN 2:2 CEV

If we love someone, we nurture the relationship. We might even sacrifice our own desires simply to make our loved one happy. Because of love, Jesus sacrificed His life on the cross to establish our relationship with His heavenly Father. Christ's death and resurrection show how far God will go to call us into relationship and keep us in there with Him. We should take pleasure in our relationship with Him because He nurtures it with His love.

Day 292
Powerful Prayer

In [God] you have been enriched in every way—
with all kinds of speech and with all knowledge.

1 Corinthians 1:5

Ask God to show you where you are not using the potential your faith has given you. Consider the things you already know about God and His commandments, and use your knowledge to introduce others to God's love. List your abilities—you have more than you think!—and consciously put them to serve others. Use your Spirit-given potential to walk as an effective, exciting, and powerful woman of God.

Day 293
"Yes!"

Everything that was written in the past was written to teach us. The Scriptures give us patience and encouragement so that we can have hope.

ROMANS 15:4 NCV

At the beginning of a romantic relationship, we might wonder if a man's feelings for us are as strong as ours are for him. In our relationship with God, however, we have our answer right away. God has revealed His attitude toward us in the words of scripture so we never have to wonder if He loves us, or guess whether He listens to our prayers. His "Yes!" rings throughout scripture, because He wants us to live with certainty of His love, peace, and protection.

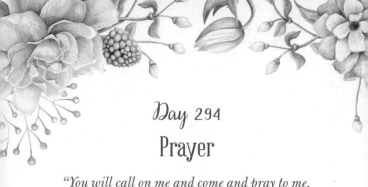

Day 294
Prayer

*"You will call on me and come and pray to me,
and I will listen to you. You will seek me and
find me when you seek me with all your heart."*

JEREMIAH 29:12–13

You may have heard many differing opinions on the subject of prayer. What God says about prayer, however, is simple. When you pray—whether kneeling, sitting, or standing; whether in time-tested words or in your own words—He hears you. He responds in a way designed to increase your faith and develop a strong relationship with Him. Continue to pray and pray faithfully, because through prayer, God offers you the comfort of daily conversation between your heart and His.

Day 295

Glowing with Good Health

*Your word is a lamp to my
feet and a light to my path.*

PSALM 119:105 NRSV

Daily scripture reading is like maintaining a healthy diet. We may not remember every one of our meals, yet we're healthier because of them. When we read and meditate on the Bible, God's words to us, the Holy Spirit strengthens our faith and nourishes us with a deeper understanding of God's will for our lives. We may not remember everything we read (or even what we read this morning!), but our hearts and souls will glow with good health.

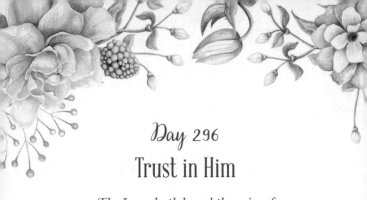

Day 296

Trust in Him

*The LORD hath heard the voice of
my weeping. The LORD hath heard my
supplication; the LORD will receive my prayer.*

PSALM 6:8–9 KJV

When you don't receive what you've prayed for, it's easy to conclude God is telling you no. Not so! He has promised to hear your prayers, but are you listening for His answer? If He chooses to not give you exactly what you have prayed for, He has chosen something better for you. If He chooses to remain silent today, He is encouraging you to continue praying, placing your trust in Him and His wisdom.

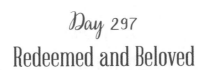

Day 297

Redeemed and Beloved

*God loved us so much that he made
us alive with Christ, and God's
wonderful kindness is what saves you.*

EPHESIANS 2:4–5 CEV

"Know yourself." In the Bible, God describes how He wants us to think, speak, and act so we will realize we cannot live up to His desires. At the same time, God expresses His love for us and outlines His plan of salvation for us so we're able to see ourselves as redeemed and beloved women of God. When we know ourselves as God knows us, we can live at peace with Him, with others, and with ourselves.

Day 298
Priorities

Fear God and obey his commands,
for this is everyone's duty.

ECCLESIASTES 12:13 NLT

Knowing God gives you a new perspective on your work, family life, and friendships. You see these God-given blessings for what they are, and you want to tend to them mindfully and well. Like a broad umbrella, however, God stands over and above you and all He has given you. Never let anything in your life take priority over God, who shelters you with His continuing guidance, comfort, and care.

Day 299

Whose We Are

Thank you for making me so wonderfully complex!
Your workmanship is marvelous—how well I know it.

PSALM 139:14 NLT

Self-awareness requires us to recognize our weaknesses and invites us to thank God for our strengths. When we celebrate our unique God-given strengths by naming them, developing them, and using them for our good and the good of others, we begin to see ourselves as gifted, talented, and capable women. Our confidence grows as our self-awareness deepens, centered in knowing who we are and, even more importantly, *whose* we are.

Day 300
First Place

Seek his will in all you do, and he will show you which path to take.

PROVERBS 3:6 NLT

Financial troubles, medical issues, relationship problems, and similar difficulties tend to occupy first place in thoughts, time, and energy. Yet this is exactly the time your priorities need to be in order! If you allow a crisis to dominate, anxiety continues to consume you, and you lose sight of the help, strength, and solace you have in God. Whether things are going smoothly or not so smoothly, make sure God stays first in your life.

Day 301
Serving Others

*"Anyone who wants to serve me must
follow me, because my servants must
be where I am. And the Father will
honor anyone who serves me."*

JOHN 12:26 NLT

No matter where we are in life, God grants us the privilege of serving Him by serving others. As we embrace God's principle of sharing as our own, we come to experience life in a whole new way. As we follow the Holy Spirit's promptings in choosing our life's direction, we discover life's purpose. Others may not understand why we have set our sights on service, but we will as we experience genuine joy and heart-deep peace.

Day 302
Protection

I've run to you for dear life. I'm hiding out under
your wings until the hurricane blows over.

<small>PSALM 57:1 MSG</small>

When bad things happen, we tend to wonder, *Isn't God supposed to protect us from disaster?* Rest assured your God knows and cares about what is taking place in your life, and His arms of comfort and consolation are there to enfold you in His love. All the while, His Holy Spirit is working in you to guard and keep your soul from anything that would threaten your eternal salvation. Hold firmly to God, and discover your immediate solace and your ultimate safety in Him.

Day 303
God Serves

There are different ways to serve the same Lord.

1 Corinthians 12:5 cev

As God serves us, we serve others. If we're in a humble position, we serve by taking genuine pleasure in our ability to help, assist, cheer, and encourage others. If we're in an influential position, we serve by speaking and acting on behalf of others, promoting fairness for all, and living as an example for others to follow. But service doesn't always come easy, and that's why God serves us each day with His wisdom, strength, and love.

Day 304
A Refuge

The eternal God is your refuge,
and underneath are the everlasting arms.

DEUTERONOMY 33:27

God's commandments always work to protect your soul and very often your mind, emotions, and body from danger. He sets His guidelines under you to keep you away from anything capable of stealing the good in your life and covering you with guilt, pain, and regret. Pray for a deeper appreciation of the refuge He has set for you in His commandments and will for your life.

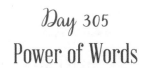

Day 305

Power of Words

Gracious words are a honeycomb,
sweet to the soul and healing to the bones.

PROVERBS 16:24

For most of us, speaking comes easy. So easy, in fact, that we forget the power of the words we use when talking to others. Just as words can convey love, kindness, care, and compassion, they can also provoke anger, cause hurt feelings, and bring offense. God's Spirit working in us prompts us to choose our words with their power in mind, using them to give thanks to God and bless the lives of others.

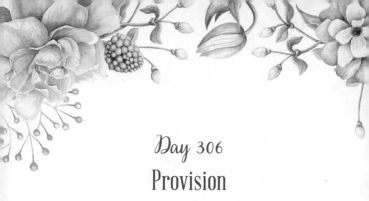

Day 306

Provision

[God] gives food to those who fear him;
he always remembers his covenant.

PSALM 111:5 NLT

We serve a God of miracles, and sometimes, miracles
come in the simplest provisions—food enough for the
next meal, a warm coat for your child, a place to sleep
at night. When the checkbook gets low and the bills are
stacking up, He is there to point you to help, to see that
you and yours have the basic needs of daily living. Thank
Him for both the small miracles and the great ones.

Day 307

His Name

*"Good people have good things in their hearts,
and so they say good things."*

MATTHEW 12:35 NCV

If we were to hear a loved one insulted, we'd feel justifiably angry. Yet when we use God's name frivolously and uselessly, we insult His Spirit dwelling within us. The twinge of guilt or nervous laughter that follows reminds us that we love God and respect His name and His holiness. No matter how often we hear it or who uses it, profanity has no place in our speech as God's beloved, forgiven, and gentle-tongued women.

Day 308

Plenty to Share

God will generously provide all you need.
Then you will always have everything you
need and plenty left over to share with others.

2 Corinthians 9:8 nlt

In a culture replete with consumer goods, the line between needs and wants tends to blur not only in ads and commercials, but in our thoughts as well. God's mind, however, is clear on the subject of needs and wants—He knows the difference. Trust Him to give you those things He knows you need, and give thanks to Him for all He provides. If you think about it, you'll realize He has given you plenty to share with others too!

Day 309
Victory

*Thank God for letting our Lord
Jesus Christ give us the victory!*
1 Corinthians 15:57 cev

We don't associate struggle with peace, but God does. In our spiritual struggle with temptations like doubt, envy, intolerance, impatience, and anger, God reminds us that His Son, Jesus, has won the victory for us. Jesus overcame temptation of all kinds, enabling us to lean on Him during our own battles. With His Spirit at work in our hearts and minds, we struggle, but we already know the outcome. We can do the impossible: struggle against sin, yet remain confident of winning!

Day 310
Purpose

We are God's handiwork, created in
Christ Jesus to do good works, which God
prepared in advance for us to do.

EPHESIANS 2:10

Some people say life is merely a meaningless accident of nature. Perhaps the idea has entered your mind and thoughts too. If so, you understand why God in His Word declares repeatedly the value He places on human life. He created you out of His eternal love, and He has made you who you are and placed you where you are for His divine purpose. Open your heart and spirit to take hold of the great purpose God has for your life.

Day 311

Mightier Than Temptation

*The temptations in your life are no different from
what others experience. And God. . .will not allow
the temptation to be more than you can stand.*

1 CORINTHIANS 10:13 NLT

The best way to meet temptation is with God's Word. In
the Bible, we discover others who have struggled with
the same things now burdening us, and we find God's
assurance of strength, power, and ultimate victory. His
promises support us with wisdom and insight, shield
us with Spirit-fed confidence, and build up our faith to
withstand the lure of temptation. Receive lasting peace
in knowing God is mightier than any temptation to sin.

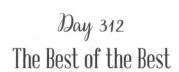

Day 312
The Best of the Best

We constantly pray for you, that our God may make you worthy of his calling, and that by his power he may bring to fruition your every desire for goodness and your every deed prompted by faith.

2 THESSALONIANS 1:11

If you could plan the course of your children's lives, would you doom them to failure and despair? Of course not. You love your children. Your plans for them would be all good. Your heavenly Father feels the same about you. And He does have the power to set in place a plan and purpose for your life. You can be certain that His will includes only the best for you—the best of joy, of love, of peace, of abundance, of success.

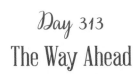

Day 313
The Way Ahead

"Don't lose your courage or be afraid.
Don't panic or be frightened, because
the LORD your God goes with you."

DEUTERONOMY 20:3-4 NCV

Starting over after misfortune takes courage, especially when we're not quite sure how to proceed. Our times of prayer and meditation take on an added importance, because we realize that only God's guiding Spirit can show us the way ahead. We want to listen and learn. We want to do the right thing, and just knowing He is there gives us the fortitude we need to confidently enter this new chapter of our lives.

Day 314

Questions

On the day I called, You answered me;
You made me bold with strength in my soul.
PSALM 138:3 NASB

"What is this?" "Where are we now?" "How come this is this way?" One thing children know how to do is ask questions. Mothers know, however, that their children might not be ready or able to hear the answers to all their questions, so they answer the ones they can and tuck the others away. Your heavenly Father hears your questions, all of them. But He doesn't give you all the answers at once. Trust Him to know what you can handle. Answer in faith.

Day 315
Back on the Path

Create in me a pure heart, O God,
and renew a steadfast spirit within me.

PSALM 51:10

Not one of us travels in a straight, smooth line to spiritual maturity. As long as we live this side of heaven, we'll stumble, fall down, and wander into dangerous places. Then when we realize our mistake and turn to God for forgiveness, our heavenly Father rushes in to pick us up, dust us off, and set us back on our path. Yes, we're stronger now, and wiser. With a hug and a smile, our God lets us start over.

Day 316
Answers

*"Call to me and I will answer you and tell you great
and unsearchable things you do not know."*

JEREMIAH 33:3

If you have ever worked with children, you know they
will sometimes ask a question but not listen to your
answer. As God's child, avoid doing the same thing.
Pose your questions to God, and then listen to His
answer. You may not like what you hear—it may be
difficult to accept or sound unreasonable to you. Ask
the Holy Spirit to deepen your understanding and
give you the power to accept even the most difficult of
God's unsearchable answers.

Day 317
God Knows

Be glad for the chance to suffer as Christ suffered.
It will prepare you for even greater happiness
when he makes his glorious return.

1 PETER 4:13 CEV

When we pour out our hearts to God, we are speaking to one who knows suffering. Our heavenly Father experienced the loss of His Son when Jesus died on the cross, and Jesus suffered injustice, mistreatment, and condemnation. God the Holy Spirit suffers when souls fall into sin and refuse His rescue. We too have suffered, and perhaps we are suffering now. Even if we believe no one could possibly know how we feel, consider this: God knows. And He also knows that happiness is just around the corner.

Day 318
Honor

A kindhearted woman gains honor.

PROVERBS 11:16

When you consistently show kindness and caring for others, sincerely honoring their humanity, their work, and their rights, you gain their honor and respect. They cannot help but notice the respect you offer to everyone, from the lowliest person to the highest, from the youngest to the oldest, from the weakest to the most powerful. Ask the Holy Spirit to help you show heartfelt honor and respect to others, because this is the way you gain respect in return.

Day 319
His Soothing Presence

Even in my suffering I was comforted
because your promise gave me life.
PSALM 119:50 GNT

The first question is why. Why did this happen?
Even if we can pinpoint a likely cause, however, our
suffering remains. So God answers our "why?" not
with an explanation, but with His soothing presence,
His compassion and understanding, and His assurance that He is still in control. Our faith matters, and
God invites us to put our trust in Him. Our feelings
matter too and God yearns to bring us His comfort
and peace.

Day 320

Building Respect

Make it your ambition to lead a quiet life:
You should mind your own business and work
with your hands, just as we told you, so that your
daily life may win the respect of outsiders and
so that you will not be dependent on anybody.

1 THESSALONIANS 4:11–12

Who you are in public and in private shapes your character and the perception people have about you. Do you consistently act in a way deserving of others' respect? Do your words and actions put others in the best light? Ask the Holy Spirit to show you what you could change to heighten the respect others have for you and to build respect for the presence of God in your life.

Day 321
Wide Open

You may make your plans,
but God directs your actions.

PROVERBS 16:9 GNT

The opportunity is gone. It's as if someone has slammed a door and it's closed tight. We can't help but stand and stare, trying to understand what happened. And our compassionate God stands right beside us. When we're ready to let Him, He will turn the eyes of our spirit to another door, this one open to us—wide open. The moment we surrender our will to the will of our loving God, we can discover all that's waiting there for us.

Day 322
Responsibility

To do what is right and just is more
acceptable to the LORD than sacrifice.

PROVERBS 21:3

Whether or not God ever calls you to make a huge personal sacrifice for Him, He definitely calls you to take on the responsibilities He has placed in front of you. These responsibilities may not differ in essence from anyone else's responsibilities, but your willing and uncomplaining acceptance of them marks you as His child. Perform them to the best of your ability, and in all you do, do the right thing.

Day 323
Room for Serenity

Be still, and know that I am God.
PSALM 46:10 KJV

God yearns to fill us with His peace, but He often finds us reluctant to give up those things that hinder it. Things like gossip and status-seeking, competition and self-centeredness, busyness and insistence on our own way. If we let God's Spirit sweep these things away from our hearts and minds, there's room for serenity to move in. If we surrender ourselves to God's overwhelming love, our spirits are ready to receive His all-consuming and everlasting peace.

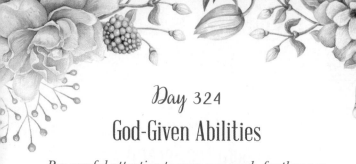

Day 324
God-Given Abilities

Pay careful attention to your own work, for then you will get the satisfaction of a job well done, and you won't need to compare yourself to anyone else. For we are each responsible for our own conduct.

GALATIANS 6:4–5 NLT

God has loaded you with more responsibilities than you can handle—or so you think! In fact, He never gives you responsibilities without also giving you the strength to manage your tasks well. When you feel overwhelmed, don't focus on getting out from under your responsibilities. Instead ask the Holy Spirit to build you up in faith and attentiveness so you can carry your own load with dignity and a true appreciation of your God-given abilities.

Day 325
Opportunity

*My brothers and sisters, when you have many
kinds of troubles, you should be full of joy.*

JAMES 1:2 NCV

God works for our good and turns even sinful desires to
our benefit. When temptation comes our way, it's yet
another opportunity for us to choose His commandments
over our urges, and another chance to put into action
our love for Him. Our Spirit-strengthened resistance
shields us from spiritual danger and enables us to gain
self-control and self-assurance. Temptation may trouble
us, but deep peace is ours when we let Him turn our
temptation to our gain.

Day 326
Rest

[Jesus said]: "Are you tired? Worn out? Burned out on religion? Come to me. Get away with me and you'll recover your life. I'll show you how to take a real rest."

<small>MATTHEW 11:28 MSG</small>

You know how it is. Busy schedules and pressure to perform crowd in on every side. But God never intended for you to be spent and weary in body and soul. Not only does He permit us to rest; He insists on it. Ask God to show you where you can open up some time to rest your body and nourish your soul, time to close your eyes, and relax in His comforting arms.

Day 327
He Leads

We are instructed to turn from godless living and
sinful pleasures. We should live in this evil world
with wisdom, righteousness, and devotion to God.

TITUS 2:12 NLT

The longer we meditate on God's will and purpose
for our lives, the more aware we become of things that
pull us away from Him. In the light of God's desires
for us, behaviors we never saw as harmful before, now
show up as hindrances to spiritual growth. Giving in
to "harmless" temptations no longer satisfies us, and
there are changes we want to make. This is God's Spirit
in us, speaking, and with His words, He leads.

Day 328

God-Given Rest

Rest in the LORD,
and wait patiently for Him.

PSALM 37:7 NKJV

You need more than rest for your body. Your mind and emotions also need to be renewed. God understands how difficult it is to step away when so many people are depending on you. Ask Him to help you find respites in the storms of life, special times, however brief, when you can rest your body and soul. Listen as He says, "Come My weary daughter, and I will give you rest."

Day 329
Wonders

*[God] gives strength to the weary
and increases the power of the weak.*

ISAIAH 40:29

Who among us doesn't know what it's like to be tired—really tired? When fatigue becomes a constant companion, it's time to find a reliable source of refreshment and relaxation. God's Spirit can do wonders when given even five or ten minutes a day to remind us of God's power in our lives and His willingness to help us with our needs and priorities. Tiredness slips away when we place our burdens on Him and lean on His ever-present strength.

Day 330

Restoration

" 'I will restore you to health and
heal your wounds,' declares the LORD."

JEREMIAH 30:17

Have you prayed many times for God's restoring hand in your life, and yet you can't seem to get over those memories and emotions that cause you so much pain? God's healing sometimes happens overnight, but most often it takes time. Take comfort in knowing that each day in some small way, He is bringing you through, giving you strength, creating for you a future based on His love.

Day 331

Spiritual Refreshment

It is useless for you to work so hard from early morning until late at night. . . for God gives rest to his loved ones.

Psalm 127:2 nlt

Tiredness tells us it's time to get some rest. Yes, each of us has a limit, both physically and emotionally. Our gracious God, creator of body and spirit, uses tiredness for our good. It's His way of drawing us to Him so He can refresh us spiritually and His way of turning us to others for relaxation, spontaneity, laughter, and friendship. We may not like to feel tired, but sometimes it's the only way God can reach us when we're on the go!

Day 332

Spiritual Gifts

The God of all grace, who called you to his eternal glory in Christ, after you have suffered a little while, will himself restore you and make you strong, firm and steadfast.

1 PETER 5:10

No matter how low your sufferings may have brought you, God works to lift you up and build you up. He is a God who takes no pleasure in seeing you broken in body or in spirit, but He takes great pleasure in restoring you and filling you with more of His spiritual gifts of patience, faith, and strength of character. Lift your eyes to God's unchangeable promise to heal you, and keep your trust in Him.

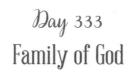

Day 333

Family of God

*Let us not neglect our meeting together,
as some people do, but encourage one another.*

HEBREWS 10:25 NLT

Year after year we celebrate treasured traditions with family and friends. As members of God's family of believers, we are blessed with many opportunities to celebrate together. Shared worship surrounds us with the encouragement and love of other believers, and holidays like Christmas and Easter offer a special chance to lift our hearts and voices together in songs of praise. When we celebrate our spiritual traditions, we share together the joy of belonging to the family of God.

Day 334
Reward

[Jesus said,] "Blessed are you when people insult you, persecute you and falsely say all kinds of evil against you because of me. Rejoice and be glad, because great is your reward in heaven."

MATTHEW 5:11–12

Though it seems noble to say, "I'm not doing this for a reward," Jesus promises a sure and certain reward to those who follow Him in obedience. His promise works to comfort you when your commitment to Him makes you the object of insult, ridicule, or slander. Don't let these things take away your peace, but instead be glad. Let insults remind you: Great is your reward in heaven.

Day 335
Inward Strength

I consider that our present sufferings are not worth
comparing with the glory that will be revealed in us.
ROMANS 8:18

We're powerless to change the situation, or the consequences of doing so are unacceptable. This kind of
trial forces us inward, where we're likely to find more
strength than we ever knew we possessed. Daily time
with God to focus on the issue renews our commitment
to a God-pleasing response in the things we think,
say, and do. Our patience amid such trials builds
resilience, and our serenity in trying times works for
peace wherever peace may find a willing heart.

Day 336
Eternal Rewards

You know that the Lord will reward each one for whatever good they do.

EPHESIANS 6:8

Through the ministry of Jesus Christ, God has done for you what you could never do for yourself—secure your salvation. He has satisfied your greatest need. Now His Holy Spirit working in you prompts you to do the things He invites His followers to do. That is, show compassion, give practical assistance to those in need, share your spiritual wisdom and understanding. He even offers you an incentive—eternal reward from your Lord and God.

Day 337
Richly Blessed

*[The Lord] said to me, "My grace is
sufficient for you, for My strength
is made perfect in weakness."*

2 Corinthians 12:9 nkjv

There are disturbing thoughts, unfortunate personality traits, or seemingly unbreakable habits or addictions. Even in trials of heart, mind, and emotions, our Great Physician is there. He opens His arms to us and invites us to rest in His peace. We discover that despite our personal burdens, God calls us His beloved daughters. His Spirit works within us and blesses us richly. We find our strength in Him alone as we walk on with Him to victory.

Day 338
Peaceful Hearts

The fruit of that righteousness will be peace;
its effect will be quietness and confidence forever.
ISAIAH 32:17

Peace begins from within, and where there's anger, violence, hatred, and fighting, there is no peace. That's why God's Spirit works in our hearts to root out those things that make our inner peace impossible. Then, with His genuine peace firmly established within us, we cannot help but express His sublime gift in our homes, communities, and workplaces. A world where each heart possesses His peace is the surest road to a world at peace.

Day 339

Companionship

Those who know your name put their trust in you,
for you, O LORD, have not forsaken those who seek you.

PSALM 9:10 NRSV

Very often we find it difficult to trust: We have been
hurt too many times. Yet lack of trust keeps us from
the close, comfortable relationships we long for. God's
Spirit draws us toward others because He desires companionship for us as we walk our life's path. He wants
only peace for us as He brings the right people alongside us, who can help and support, encourage, and
love us as we learn to trust again.

Day 340

God's Definition of Work

We are what he has made us, created in
Christ Jesus for good works, which God
prepared beforehand to be our way of life.

EPHESIANS 2:10 NRSV

Deadlines and long to-do lists, endless chores and household demands all give work a bad name! Yet God intends our work to not only provide for our needs and the needs of others, but to bring us a sense of fulfillment and satisfaction. When we go to Him and "unload" at the end of the day, God makes it His work to help and support us and enable us to make His definition of work a reality in our lives.

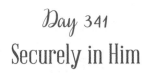

Day 341

Securely in Him

*I trust in your love. My heart is happy
because you saved me. I sing to the
LORD because he has taken care of me.*

PSALM 13:5–6 NCV

When we trust someone it shows in our actions. We can
depend on and confide in that person without worry
of betrayal. Our trust in God expresses itself in action
too. Trust compels us to rely on His promises and take
Him at His word when He says He'll bless us, strengthen
us, and comfort us. Trust in God enables us to live at
peace with Him, with ourselves, and with others,
because our faith rests securely in Him.

Day 342

Service

There are different kinds
of service, but the same Lord.

1 CORINTHIANS 12:5

Even after you commit yourself to following God's will, jealousy can creep into your heart. You notice her work gets so much more recognition than yours and her gifts seem so much greater. God would have you turn from the temptation to compare your work with anyone else's. Both of you in your different roles serve the same God. Put your confidence in Him as you serve Him and others in every way open to you.

Day 343

Free Hearts

[God] has rescued us from the power of darkness and transferred us into the kingdom of his beloved Son, in whom we have redemption, the forgiveness of sins.

COLOSSIANS 1:13–14 NRSV

Peace and violence do not go together, and God is a God of peace. To the tears of violence, He brings His words of comfort and compassion, and to the wounds of violence, He brings the balm of emotional and spiritual healing. To the scars of violence, He enables forgiveness. Through forgiveness, violence loses its power to inflict more harm. Forgiveness frees our hearts and minds to live again as women worthy of honor, dignity, and love.

Day 344

Opportunities to Serve

*[Jesus said,] "Whoever serves me must follow
me; and where I am, my servant also will be.
My Father will honor the one who serves me."*

JOHN 12:26

Following Jesus requires you to serve others wherever
you are. Never for a moment wait for other circumstances, a more convenient time, a later date! The
moment you commit yourself to following Jesus
Christ, you give yourself to serving others by showing
compassion and kindness, by offering help and counsel,
by bringing His love wherever you are right now. Pray
for His Spirit to open your eyes to see opportunities
to serve Him.

Day 345
Peaceful Hearts

The fruit of that righteousness will be peace;
its effect will be quietness and confidence forever.

ISAIAH 32:17

Peace begins from within, and where there's anger, violence, hatred, and fighting, there is no peace. That's why God's Spirit works in our hearts to root out those things that make our inner peace impossible. Then, with His genuine peace firmly established within us, we cannot help but express His sublime gift in our homes, communities, and workplaces. A world where each heart possesses His peace is the surest road to a world at peace.

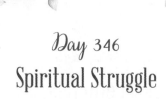

Day 346
Spiritual Struggle

*Put on the full armor of God, so that you can take
your stand against the devil's schemes. For our
struggle is not against flesh and blood, but against
the rulers, against the authorities, against the
powers of this dark world and against the
spiritual forces of evil in the heavenly realms.*

Ephesians 6:11–12

You cannot fight temptation on your own. Deadly
spiritual forces work to pull you away from God and
into the grip of sin, turmoil, and despair. Pray for a
realistic awareness of the forces fighting against you,
and let the Holy Spirit equip you for the struggle. Fill
your mind and heart with His Word, dedicate yourself to listening only to the still, small voice of God
inside you, and rely on His power and strength.

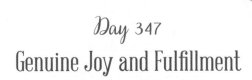

Day 347
Genuine Joy and Fulfillment

Surely the LORD your God has
blessed you in all your undertakings.

DEUTERONOMY 2:7 NRSV

All honest work pleases God. Unlike the world around us, God does not judge on status or pay scale, or on whether our work takes us around the world or no farther than our kitchen sink. Instead, God looks at our hearts, where He delights to find integrity, patience, honesty, and trustworthiness. He knows that from this heart genuine joy flows, and wherever joy is present, there is fulfillment in work and peace in spirit.

Day 348
Give Thanks!

Pursue righteousness, godliness,
faith, love, endurance and gentleness.
Fight the good fight of the faith.

1 TIMOTHY 6:11–12

Through your faith, God's Spirit has put into your heart the vision of His will for your life. It's like a precious gift inside you, building you up and giving you the desire and motivation you need to fight for your spiritual life. Keep doing the right thing, continue learning, and persist in praying that your faith will grow and strengthen in the struggle. Spiritual warfare is happening because you've moved away from the grip of wickedness and into the arms of God. Give thanks!

Day 349
You're Equipped

In Christ you have been brought to fullness.
He is the head over every power and authority.

COLOSSIANS 2:10

Do you feel incomplete or inadequate, unable to carry out the tasks God has given you? You aren't, you know, if you tap into His Spirit. God equips you to do all things in Him. If you feel overwhelmed, make sure you haven't taken on tasks rightfully belonging to someone else. God does not overload your life with busyness. He has a purpose for all you do. So be certain you're serving in the right place, doing the work He planned for you.

Day 350
Starting Over

This is what the LORD says—your Redeemer,
the Holy One of Israel: . . . "For I am about
to do something new. See, I have already
begun! Do you not see it?"

ISAIAH 43:14, 19 NLT

When the Holy Spirit brought you to faith in Jesus Christ, your life started over. You may or may not have realized it at the time, and since then you might have slid right back into doing things the same old way and thinking the same old thoughts. Your new life in Christ, however, is not a onetime event. It happens each time you come to Him and ask for renewal and refreshment. Seek Him, and start over again today.

Day 351
Worthy Traditions

The LORD is good and his love endures forever;
his faithfulness continues through all generations.

PSALM 100:5

All too often, the holidays we celebrate turn into times of tension and stress. It's through Spirit-inspired decision and action that we can reshape our holiday traditions. We can focus on what's meaningful to us and the people we love, and we can decline to participate in those things that drain our time and energy. Through our efforts, we can establish traditions that bless us—traditions worthy to be passed down to the next generation.

Day 352
A Clean Slate

Create in me a pure heart, God,
and make my spirit right again.

PSALM 51:10 NCV

The psalmist had strayed so far from God's will for his life that he dropped to his knees and prayed for a whole new heart and spirit. If you have strayed, you can join the psalmist in his plea. Ask God to give you a clean heart, a restored spirit, and a chance to walk with Him again. Trust in Him to forgive you, and you will see the miracle of a brand-new life.

Day 353
Support and Strength

Unto you that fear my name shall the Sun of righteousness arise with healing in his wings.

MALACHI 4:2 KJV

We're nothing like the beaming mother-to-be on the magazine cover. Our roller-coaster emotions and aching backs tell a whole different story! But our Great Physician is always there, inviting us to remember His compassion and love as we entrust our health and well-being to Him. We can ask Him for the support we need, and receive it in abundance through the strength He gives us and the help He provides through the hearts and hands of others.

Day 354
Strength

*I can do all this through
him who gives me strength.*
PHILIPPIANS 4:13

Has a new opportunity opened for you? Maybe after
thinking and praying about it, you feel drawn to take on
the project, but a nagging doubt holds you back. Are
you strong enough? If you keep looking at your own
strength, you will pass on the opportunity. If instead
you look to God and realize it's His strength He's
offering, you can take on the challenge with confidence.
In Him, you have great strength!

Day 355

Hope for Tomorrow

He comforts us every time we have trouble,
so when others have trouble, we can comfort
them with the same comfort God gives us.

2 Corinthians 1:4 ncv

Loss hurts, and it's important for us to recognize our pain and open ourselves to God's comfort and to the consolation of others. While nothing can take the place of what has been lost, the promises of God offer us hope for tomorrow, and the presence of friends and loved ones supports us in our grief. We were never meant to bear loss alone, but to walk hand in hand through sorrow, with our footsteps following His will and purpose.

Day 356

He Is Strong

The Lord is faithful, and he will strengthen
you and protect you from the evil one.

2 Thessalonians 3:3

God never expects you to hold on to your faith by your own strength. He knows the weakness of all human hearts, and He knows all about the temptations you deal with every day. With His own strength, God will defend you! Ask the Holy Spirit to give you His strength and power, so you will exercise your spiritual muscles and move beyond your frailty. Where you are weak, God is strong.

Day 357
Lift Us Up

Peace of mind makes the body healthy.
PROVERBS 14:30 GNT

Sickness attacks our bodies and weighs down our hearts. But no matter how low we feel, God's presence is there to lift us up. Perhaps even more clearly than when we're in great health, we hear His words of comfort and sense His touch of consolation and renewal. The Great Physician desires to reveal Himself to us in these trying times so we will know that His peace is ours, His love is real, all the time.

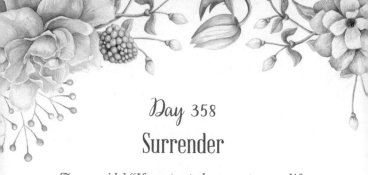

Day 358

Surrender

*[Jesus said,] "If you try to hang on to your life,
you will lose it. But if you give up your life for my sake
and for the sake of the Good News, you will save it."*

MARK 8:35 NLT

You may have thought about the concept of surrendering yourself to God, but you've hesitated because you want to be who you are—not a puppet of someone else. Don't worry! After all, God is the one who created you to be the unique woman you are. He has no intention of tampering with that. His goal is just to offer stability in your emotions and thought life and to enhance your talents and abilities. Surrender to the hand of God means fulfillment of your deepest God-given desires.

Day 359

God at the Center

*Let the mighty strength of
the Lord make you strong.*
EPHESIANS 6:10 CEV

Where family ties are strongest, God dwells at the center of the household. He yearns to be the one we turn to when pressures and problems arise, and when arguments threaten to alienate spouses, parents, and children. If forgiveness seems difficult, God can smooth the way. If old wounds still fester, God can provide healing and comfort. Strong families aren't built by human effort alone but by God's power and presence in our homes.

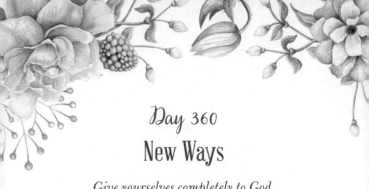

Day 360
New Ways

Give yourselves completely to God.
Stand against the devil, and the devil
will run from you. Come near to God,
and God will come near to you.

James 4:7–8 ncv

Sometimes when we aren't entirely convinced we want to go all out for God, we try to keep Him at a safe distance. Yet to go all out for Him is what God is asking each of us to do. He knows how hesitance keeps us vulnerable to the pull of doubt, the fear of life, and the pain of reverting back to our old ways. Let Him close the distance between you. You will be amazed by how comforting it can be to be fully surrendered to Him.

Day 361
Embraced in Love

The LORD is good, a refuge in times of trouble.
He cares for those who trust in him.

NAHUM 1:7

Sometimes our friendships and marriages fail us. Sometimes we even fail ourselves when we don't live up to our standards or reach our goals. Yet even in failure, God soothes us with His presence and embraces us in His love. He's not there to judge or point a finger, but only to support us through a rough part of the road and lead us in the direction He would have us go. Real failure would be to refuse His help.

Day 362
Temptation

Because [Jesus] himself suffered when he was tempted, he is able to help those who are being tempted.

HEBREWS 2:18

Jesus has passed this way ahead of you. In His humanity, He was tempted and He knows firsthand its power and pull. He has compassion on the weakness of human flesh, and He is not ashamed to travel with you in your struggle. He wants you to live free, without the tentacles and restrictions of destructive behaviors and unhealthy desires. The challenge is great, but He has promised to walk with you, comforting and strengthening you every step of the way.

Day 363

In Harmony

"Do not be afraid of their words
or dismayed by their looks."

EZEKIEL 2:6 NKJV

No matter how hard we try to live in harmony with others, there may be individuals or groups determined to do us harm. While we remain watchful, defending ourselves if attacked by our enemies, God would have us do something else, and that is pray for them. We pray for His Spirit of love to soften their hearts and enlighten their minds, because in Him alone is true and lasting peace among people and among nations.

Day 364
Time

There is a right time and a
right way for everything.

ECCLESIASTES 8:6 NCV

Pure and simple, time is a gift. Each second, minute, hour, and day are yours to use as you please. *Not so fast,* you might be thinking. *All my time is filled with work and responsibilities and taking care of other people.* That's true, your time might be dictated by other choices you have made, but it is still yours. Ask God to help you squeeze in some time for yourself. He'll show you where to find it.

Day 365

Refreshing Waters

You must get rid of all these things: anger,
passion, and hateful feelings. No insults or
obscene talk must ever come from your lips.

COLOSSIANS 3:8 GNT

While going through a divorce is painful, allowing
resentment to linger in our lives is worse. Resentment can
last for years, decades, and beyond within the heart that
harbors it, poisoning present and future relationships,
and undermining self-confidence and inner peace.
Genuine, heart-deep forgiveness is the only remedy
for the bitterness, hurt, anger, and animosity divorce
so commonly leaves in its wake. With forgiveness, the
refreshing waters of renewal flow into a cleansed and
blameless heart.

Read Thru the Bible
in a Year Plan

More Encouragement to Uplift Your Spirit

Writing Peace on My Heart

Here is a 6-week devotional that focuses on one simple Bible memory verse per week. Equal parts challenging and encouraging, this unique book includes 6 full-color, tear-out index cards, each with a weekly memory verse printed on it to be displayed as a reminder to write God's Word on your heart—perfect for the fridge, bathroom mirror, computer monitor, or even as a bookmark.

Paperback / 978-1-64352-879-3 / $9.99

180 Prayers for a Woman of Confidence

This devotional prayer book is a powerful reminder to confidently bring any petition before your heavenly Father. Dozens of just-right-sized prayers touch on topics that will resonate with your heart. Topics include: True Beauty, Self-Worth, Boldness, Trust, and more.

Paperback / 978-1-64352-865-6 / $4.99